A GRIM ALMANAC OF

LANCASHIRE

A GRIM ALMANAC OF

LANCASHIRE

JACK NADIN

The History Press

First published 2011

The History Press
The Mill, Brimscombe Port
Stroud, Gloucestershire, GL5 2QG
www.thehistorypress.co.uk

British Library Cataloguing in Publication Data.
A catalogue record for this book is available from the British Library.

ISBN 978 0 7524 5684 3

Typesetting and origination by The History Press
Printed in Great Britain
Manufacturing managed by Jellyfish Print Solutions Ltd

CONTENTS

ACKNOWLEDGEMENTS

I would like to thank all those who gave me help and assistance whilst researching this book. In particular, the staff at various libraries around the county, including those at Rawtenstall, Clitheroe, Burnley, Bury, Accrington, Blackburn, Salford and staff at Preston Records Office. I would also like to thank Alan Davies, for his help in mining-related subjects in the south of the county, and Ken Spencer, who is always willing to share his extensive knowledge of the county with those who care to listen to his wisdom. Finally, but certainly not least, my wife Rita, who in spite of her illness over the past years, bravely borne, has never complained about all the time I spent writing books – my favourite occupation.

INTRODUCTION

Lancashire's a grand old county – 'The friendliest folk in Britain are those up north', it's been said, and Lancashire has been called the most colourful county in the land; you only need to see the bright lights of Blackpool during the illuminations to know how true that is. But Lancashire has a darker side. *A Grim Almanac of Lancashire* recalls this shady history of the county's past, including tales of witchcraft and the famous Lancashire Witches, which arguably resulted in one of the biggest miscarriages of justice in British history. There are tales of murder, hangings, dreadful mining disasters, horrific mill accidents and explosions, train crashes and air disasters. There are dismal details of tragic love affairs, suicides, murderous husbands and disasters at sea. With a move away from the frequently-told stories of murders and crime in the vast cities and large towns, I have tried to include tales that shocked the smaller towns and villages in Lancashire's past. Tales of a Lancashire you never wished to know and never knew existed.

Jack Nadin, 2011

January

Worsthorne village, scene of the 1937 massacre. (*See* 27 January.)

1 JANUARY **1858** James Murray and his wife Ellen, of Radclyffe Street, Oldham, liked to have a drink or two, and both had been out celebrating New Year's Day in 1858. Ellen and her mother were making their way back to her house, when three men approached them. One of the men knocked her mother to the floor, while the other two pushed and pulled Ellen, calling her names. Ellen cried out in fear, 'Murder, murder!' and her husband rushed out to see what was going on. Ellen lifted her mother off the floor and they both went indoors. Minutes later, her husband came rushing in and accused her of an act of indecency with one of the men outside. He then beat her and kicked her, pulled her hair and knocked her down. Following this, he sharpened a knife on the kitchen slop stone and threatened to cut her throat with it. Ellen grabbed the knife and managed to get it off her husband – but not before receiving a number of wounds to her throat. James Murray was taken to court over the affair and, after hearing the evidence, the magistrate ordered that the prisoner be committed to gaol for one month.

2 JANUARY **1845** James Warburton, who kept a house of bad reputation in Hamer's Yard, near Clerk Street, Bury, was brought up on a charge of attempting to shoot a young woman named Martha Ackers, and then attempting to murder her by striking her with the butt end of the gun. The young woman was roughly 23 years of age and had lived at Warburton's house for about six weeks. One Saturday night, she entered the house and saw Warburton and an old man sat down. Warburton jumped out of his seat and pointed the gun, but it did not go off. He then struck her with the butt end, and she fell to the ground. She believed his intention was to kill her, for he came into William Walker's beerhouse in Clerk Street at about nine o'clock, and said then that he would shoot her. Eliza Walker heard him say that he would shoot Martha Ackers. Isaac Ramsden said that he had gone to Walker's beerhouse on Saturday evening, and also into the yard where Warburton resides. He had heard a noise, and, on seeing some boys run, went towards the house to see what the matter was. He saw Warburton with the gun in his hand, and heard him say that he would shoot Martha Ackers; then Warburton pointed the gun at her, and hit her several times about the head with the butt end. She fell to the ground and lay there for several minutes, bleeding very much. He was committed for trial at the next Liverpool Assizes.

3 JANUARY **1863** Thomas Edwards suffered death by hanging at Kirkdale Prison for the murder of Isabella Tonge, committed on 12 November 1862. The local newspapers described this public hanging in great detail, reporting:

On the previous Friday he [Thomas Edwards] was visited by a friend, and also by his mother and brother. Last night he could not sleep well, and engaged in constant prayer. In the morning he partook of breakfast and afterwards received the Sacrament. Shortly before twelve, Edwards was taken to the pinioning room, where he was bound by Calcraft [the hangman] and then a procession was formed, and proceeded to the scaffold. Edwards walked with a firm step, but manifested not the slightest spirit of bravado. When the culprit stood on the drop, a low moan rose from the crowds, and while the cap and rope were being adjusted by Calcraft, breathless silence prevailed. Calcraft, having completed his arrangements, shook hands with Edwards, and then retired with the chaplain. Edwards continued to say his responses, 'Lord have mercy on me – Christ have mercy on me.' Calcraft then drew the bolt and his tongue was silenced forever. Edwards being a light and strong man struggled very much ... About 8,000 to 10,000 persons – all from the lowest classes – witnessed the execution, and were looked after by a large body of police. To the discredit of some person, a drag [carriage] containing respectably dressed children was brought close to the gallows.

4 JANUARY

1911 When James Henry Bingham was appointed resident caretaker at Lancaster Castle, he was carrying on a family tradition and following in the footsteps of his recently deceased father, who was a caretaker at the castle for thirty years. James was quick to appoint his sister Margaret as housekeeper at the castle – it was then that things started to go wrong. Almost immediately, Margaret died, and she was succeeded by James's half-sister Edith Agnes Bingham. Within a few months, James Henry Bingham also died – the third family member to die within a year. James had died after eating a steak cooked by his half-sister. Suspecting foul play, the coroner at the inquest ordered that the Bingham bodies be dug up – each contained a fatal quantity of arsenic. Edith Bingham was charged with the murder of James Bingham and put on trial at the Lancaster Assizes, held by chance at Lancaster Castle, where the family had worked for generations. The court heard about the many quarrels between the brother and half-sister, and that Edith had access to weed killer for treating the castle paths and gardens. But in

Lancaster Castle has seen many hangings and trials for murder, witchcraft and other crimes.

the end nothing could actually be proved regarding Edith's connection with the death, and the case had to be dismissed after she was found 'not guilty'. A note about the case said that she then 'Retreated into obscurity'.

5 JANUARY   1851   An inquest on the body of James Farr, a labourer aged 76 years, was held at the Three Arrows Inn, Radcliffe before Mr W.S. Rutter. It appeared that the deceased was found in a well near the house of James Taylor, a beer seller, the previous Friday. He had been drinking at the house of Taylor the night before and left the house at about ten o'clock. He was never again seen alive, and was found in the well with his head downwards. Farr had had no regular home and had slept in outhouses for the last twenty years or more. A verdict of 'found drowned' was returned.

6 JANUARY   1876   There is nothing stronger than a mother's love, it is often said. However, the trauma of childbirth can have a strange effect on young mothers – take, for instance, this case in Liverpool. Elizabeth Plent was a 22-year-old servant girl living in the city, who calmly murdered her own infant by slitting its throat. She was immediately taken into custody and charged with manslaughter. In late March she was found guilty of the offence, but the jury passed on a recommendation for mercy. His Lordship, however, said he could not forget the extent to which this crime prevailed, and would pass upon the prisoner the sentence which he invariably delivered in such cases – ten years' penal servitude.

7 JANUARY   1856   Charles Whitehead was charged at Rochdale for severely beating his wife's child. On the previous Saturday night, his wife entered the police station and said that her husband was killing her child. An officer found the child's face and arms covered in blood, flowing from the nose and mouth, and there appeared to be internal injuries. Some years ago Whitehead was a serving soldier, and while he was away this child was born to his wife. On being discharged, he took an instant dislike to the girl. An elder sister gave evidence, and said that her father had come home tipsy and found the little girl asleep. He had then struck her violently on the chest and proceeded to otherwise maltreat the infant. The mother and elder sister ran out of the house in fright. Whitehead was committed to the house of correction with hard labour for six weeks.

8 JANUARY   1856   Hezekiah Heap, aged ten or eleven, was charged with stealing a measuring tape from the shop of Messrs Cowgill & Smith, ironmongers of St James Street, Burnley. He had been charged with stealing several times, but each time there was insufficient evidence to convict him. The magistrates had sent him away to the workhouse two or three times, but he ran away. The last time, he escaped over the wall within a few minutes

of entering, while the governor was still getting his clothes. When the measuring tape was found upon his person and he was charged with stealing it, the lad said, 'You will have to prove that before you can do anything to me.' The magistrates ordered for him to be imprisoned for three months, and whipped before being discharged.

1909 Two young people from Littleborough, near Rochdale went missing from their homes. They were 13-year-old William Heyworth, a cotton operative and Florence Shaw, the same age, a woollen weaver; the pair had been courting for some time. After a search was made they were found clasped in each other's arms in the Rochdale Canal near Windy Bridge. There was thick fog on the night they went missing, and it was supposed that the unfortunate pair had lost their way and unwittingly walked into the canal and drowned.

9 JANUARY

1874 Whilst a lad named William Bowker was collecting firewood, he spotted the body of a man wedged between a stone and a balk of wood in the river Irwell near Bury. He reported the matter to the police, and the body was taken out of the water. The deceased had no coat on and his shirt, waistcoat and trousers were nearly torn to pieces. In his pocket was a knife and a tin match box, but no money. The body, which appeared to have been in the water for several days, was recognised as being James Ashworth of Edge Lane near Newchurch-in-Rossendale.

10 JANUARY

Edge Lane, where James Ashworth lived. He was found floating in the river Irwell in suspicious circumstances in 1874.

He was last seen alive by his brother Robert on Monday 5 January. His sweetheart, Susannah Bridge of the Fall Barn, stated that Bowker had been to see her that afternoon at the Longholme weaving shed, Rawtenstall. He had asked to see her in the yard, and, thinking that he had been drinking, she did not go close to him. There was another man with him, a quarryman whose name she did not know. When the body was examined for the post-mortem, there was a semicircular wound 3.5in in length over the right side of his head, and from it another wound extending over the forehead. A piece of bone the size of a half crown was missing, and the scalp was detached from the skull at the top. It was believed that death was caused by a blow to the skull, and that the wounds would have made death almost instantaneous. He might have fallen from a height into the river, but there was no indication of death by drowning.

11 JANUARY **1867** Seventy-four-year-old farm labourer John Lee of Burnley went into the White Lion public house at around one o'clock and asked the landlady for some black pudding and a glass of rum. After this he went to sleep; the landlord found him the next day still asleep. He shook him and the man appeared to recognise the landlord and, at his request, had a coffee. About noon he was taken into the bar parlour by the landlord and his son, who suspected that something was not right, but before medical assistance could be obtained the man passed away. The inquest recorded a verdict of 'death by starvation' and it was stated that the deceased had no proper abode, and that he had not slept in a bed for sixteen or seventeen years.

12 JANUARY **1855** Sixty-year-old Jane Cooper was brought before Bolton magistrates on a charge of stealing a chemise, a skirt, a pillow slip, three pockets, a knife and a comb. She had been a known thief for fifteen years and was once transported for seven years. The stolen property belonged to Betty Norris and was in a cellar in Old Hall Street. The property had been secure on the previous Friday when Mrs Norris had gone to work. About two o'clock in the afternoon, Henry Rostron had seen the prisoner come out of the cellar carrying something under her shawl, and, knowing that Mrs Norris was at work, he had followed Jane and found upon her the articles named. She was committed for trial.

13 JANUARY **1846** Joseph Ward, employed at Mr Dearden's coal mine at Birtle near Bury, arrived at the pit in the early hours, entered a cabin, and opened the door of the fire grate to get it ready for the other men – but he was horrified to see a human leg there. He called for help, and, on pulling it down, discovered that it belonged to James Horrox, a man employed at the pit. Horrox was consumed almost to a cinder; his legs and arms were nearly burnt off, and the whole of the body was so disfigured that he could only be recognised by part of his shoe. He was 41 years of age and lived with his aged parents in Dawson Street, Heywood. It was thought that he wanted to go to sleep in the cabin after a heavy night's drinking and, finding the cabin door locked, had tried to gain entry by the chimney, thinking that the fire would be out – but he was burned alive.

1853   A carriage carrying Mr Moses Smith (a beer seller from Little Bolton) and his wife, his sister-in-law Miss Brandwood, another sister-in-law Mrs Brandwood, and two of her children, was going up the steep ascent near the Farmers Arms, Radcliffe Road, Darcy Lever. About 20-30 yards above the canal bridge, the horse became restive and started to back down the hill. Miss Brandwood jumped out of the carriage and managed to get one of the children out. Mrs Brandwood was attempting to follow her with the other child, when a sudden jerk threw them both out on to the highway – she had her arm broken and her wrist dislocated. Both carriage and horse were then overturned and rolled down a steep bank. Mr Smith escaped with little injury, but at the bottom of the incline Mrs Smith was found to be under the horse. When she was finally extricated she was seriously injured. The place in question is very dangerous, and a fatal accident took place there a few years ago.

14 JANUARY

The steep ascent where a poor horse was unable to cope with its heavy load and overturned, causing serious injury to Mrs Smith.

15 JANUARY

15 JANUARY **1855** Two young people, George Harrison and Dorothy Ann Ashton, were brought before the Bench at the Bolton Borough Court and charged with stealing a crown piece from a lad named Edward Kay. The lad had been sent to the shop to purchase some flour; he had a bag in his hand and a crown in his waistcoat pocket. In Deansgate, the male prisoner had approached the boy and asked him to look over a door to help him find his lost knife. The boy consented, and Harrison had lifted him up so he could look over the door, but no knife could be seen. Harrison then walked away, and the boy went forward to make his purchase – it was then that he realised the man had robbed him of the crown piece. Information was given to the police and the prisoner was traced to a lodging house where both he and Dorothy were arrested. A shopkeeper named Pendlebury proved that the female prisoner had gone into his shop on Saturday morning and paid for some groceries with a crown piece. The woman was discharged, but Harrison was committed to the New Bailey for one month as a rogue and vagabond. He had with him some false whiskers and two changes of clothing.

16 JANUARY **1832** William Howarth, aged 49, and 77-year-old John Hagan and his wife, were in the habit of sleeping in the one bed at their home in St George's Road, Withington, Manchester. In the early hours, John Hagan asked his wife if she could get him a drink of water – she went downstairs and was absent for around ten minutes, leaving the old man and William Howarth alone in the bedroom. Whilst getting the drink for her husband, she heard a groan from the upstairs bedroom, and when she returned her husband complained of being hurt, with a pain in his heart. During the following days he was in constant pain, and on the eighth day he passed away. Henry Ollier, a surgeon, examined the body of John Hagan two days after his death and found injuries near the pit of the stomach, although there were no external marks. It was his opinion that the injuries had been caused by a massive kick or blow to the area, and that was the cause of death. He also found damage to the brain, caused by a blow. Howarth was later charged with manslaughter, and at a hearing in March was sentenced to transportation for life.

17 JANUARY **1790** George McNamara was charged with being one of the men who committed a robbery at the house of Mr Chetham, the landlord of the Dog and Partridge on Stretford Road, Manchester. He was convicted at Lancaster Assizes, from where he was transferred to the New Bailey Gaol. On Saturday, 11 September 1790, he was taken by the chaplain and a large posse of police officers to Kersal Moor, where a gallows had been erected on one of the eminences. The number of spectators attracted by the novel but awful scene was immense, and, because of the location of the gallows, the inhabitants of the surrounding countryside had the opportunity to see the apparatus of death and the victim swinging on the beam.

1856   Just a few minutes before noon, a 15-year-old youth called Thomas Heaton, an apprentice at the Bradshaw Hall bleach-works, Bolton was caught by a horizontal shafting which whirled him round on the spot, killing him instantly.   18 JANUARY

1857   A locomotive boiler exploded at Sough railway station, claiming the lives of Henry Young and Daniel Greenwood. The former was a 29-year-old guard and conductor of the ballast wagons; he was taken to the infirmary in Bolton, much scalded and hurt about the body, where he died at about 3.30.   19 JANUARY

When the train arrived at Sough at about two o'clock, Greenwood, the engine driver, sent Ellis Isherwood, a stoker, under the engine to clean the fire. When he left the engine, Greenwood was putting coke upon the fire, and Young was standing close to the boiler. Isherwood had been under the engine for about three minutes when he heard a noise, and thought that a tube had burst. The engine began to move forward towards Blackburn, and Isherwood lay on the ground until the engine and tender had passed over him. He then got up and saw the deceased hanging from the tender, his feet held fast in the handrail. The firebox end of the engine had been blown out. Greenwood was lying on his back about 20 yards lower down; he had a hole in his back and his clothes were blown off – he died in about ten minutes. The safety valve blew off when the pressure reached 65; the steam blew off at Over Darwen. John Mather, a platelayer, was on one of the ballast wagons when the explosion took place. It was like the discharge of a cannon. He ran to the engine and assisted Isherwood in getting the deceased from the tender. James Tonge, foreman of the locomotive department at Bolton, said that he had known the engine for about seven years, and considered it to be in good order.

1854   An inquest was held at the Bulls Head Inn, Millgate, Spotland, on the body of Lawrence Roberts. This quarryman was killed on the previous Tuesday whilst at work in the Pisgah Bank stone pit belonging to Mr Nathan Hoyle. It appears that he was killed by a large quantity of earth falling upon him. A verdict of 'accidental death' was returned.   20 JANUARY

1833   An inquiry into the Employment of Children in Factories was conducted in 1833. Mr E.C. Tufnell stated in that inquiry that, 'The hardest labour, in the worst room, in the worst conducted factory, is less hard, less cruel, and less demoralising than the labour of the best of   21 JANUARY coal mines.' Prior to 1842 there was no age limit for the employment of children underground in coal mines. Below is a poem about a young girl who was employed in the pits around Worsley, Manchester:

The Collier Lass

My name's Polly Parker, I come o'er from Worsley
My father and mother work in the coal mine
Our family's large, we have got seven children,
So I am obliged to work in the same mine.
As this is my fortune, I know you'll feel sorry
That in such employment my days I shall pass
I keep up my spirits, I sing and look merry
Although I am but a poor collier lass.

By the greatest of dangers each day I'm surrounded
I hang in the air by a rope or a chain.
The mine may fall in, I may be killed or wounded,
May perish by damp or the fire of the train.
And what would you do if it weren't for our labour?
In wretched starvation your days you would pass,
While we could provide you with life's greatest blessing,
Then do not despise the poor collier lass.

22 JANUARY   **1851**   William Halstead, a stone mason living at Worsthorne village near Burnley, was found by his nephew suspended by his neck from a rope on a beam in his bedroom. He was last seen alive by his nephew, who had left him in bed at about eleven o'clock in the morning. No reason could be assigned to his act, and the deceased was a steady, well-conducted man in all respects. An inquest was due to be held at the Bay Horse Inn the following day.

23 JANUARY   **1854**   An accident in which five men were injured occurred at Blackburn Town Hall. Several men were working on a platform, and another labourer was wheeling a large stone upon the plank, when somehow the barrow overturned. The large stone fell upon the scaffold, breaking the putlocks, and threw the five men into the cellars below. Medical assistance was prompt, and as soon as possible the men were conveyed to their respective homes. It was later ascertained that none of the men had received any life-threatening injuries.

24 JANUARY   **1860**   An inquest was held on the body of Captain Chalmers of the schooner *Ann Mitchell* of Montrose. She left Sligo laden with oats for

Liverpool and all went well until very foul weather, including severe gales, overtook her in Morecambe Bay. The anchor was dropped but the cable snapped and the ship became unmanageable, drifting on to Bernard Bank Shoal opposite the river Wyre. The lifeboats were soon launched and managed to throw them a rope and, by this means, the mate was hauled on to the lifeboat. Another rope was thrown to the captain and two seamen. Unfortunately, they got entangled with the fallen mast and drowned, in spite of the efforts of the lifeboat men. The jury returned a verdict of 'accidentally drowned'. The body of Robert Middleton, one of the seamen, was picked up on Pilling Sands a few days later.

1865 An inquest on the death of 27-year-old Margaret Smith was **25 JANUARY** held at the Royal Hotel at Heysham. The deceased was the mother of two illegitimate children, one of whom, a girl aged 7 or 8 weeks, died on the previous Tuesday and was buried in Heysham churchyard without funeral rites, as she had not been christened. No medicines, except a little castor oil, had been given to the child, and she died very suddenly after a few hours of illness. The mother had been ill since her confinement and was attended to by Margaret Perkins, a midwife in the village. About a month before her death, she went to see Dr Irvine, but he never attended her. She got steadily worse and subsequently expired. The jury returned a verdict of 'death from natural causes'.

1869 The Fog Bell, on top of a post in Marshside Road, Southport, can **26 JANUARY** still be seen and has in recent years been renovated. It was erected to

The Fog Bell at Southport recalls the tragic events of 1869.

prevent a repeat of an accident when seven local fishermen died after becoming lost in fog on the foreshore here in January 1869. Their names were W.M. Hesketh, P. Aughton, J. Rimmer, P. Rimmer, R. Wright, J. Wright and P. Wright. The bell replaced the foghorn, which can still be seen in the Botanic Gardens at Southport.

27 JANUARY

1937   Saville Green Farm lies in the foothills of the Pennines, just above the village of Worsthorne, 3 miles from Burnley. It was home to 46-year-old farmer Foulds Wilkinson, his daughter Jane Ellen and his 73-year-old father-in-law William Pickup. Foulds employed a cowman by the name of John James Blackburn, who lived in the village, to help out around the farm. John did not last long – his time keeping left a lot to be desired and he was lazy in his work – and he was finally sacked. Foulds Wilkinson gave the job to Joseph Henry Scriven, a 30-year-old farm hand, who in fact lived next door to John James Blackburn in Worsthorne. Wednesday, 27 January 1937, was a cold frosty morning. On this day, Foulds Wilkinson drove his milk wagon out of the farmyard to do his deliveries. His father-in-law and his daughter Jane were busying themselves around the farmhouse, and the new hand, Scriven, was at his duties in the shippon. John James Blackburn was seen in the village with a sack slung over his shoulder, heading off up the hill towards Saville Green. The Wilkinsons had employed Frederick Brown to do some decorating at the farm, and

Saville Green Farm, where John James Blackburn murdered three people before turning the gun upon himself.

he had agreed to make a start that very morning. He approached Saville Green by a footpath, and was climbing over a wall when he was startled to see young Jane lying in the farmyard with her head almost in a mixing trough. He went to her aid as quickly as possible, when he suddenly saw another body – that of the old man Pickup – 5 yards from Jane. Both were beyond help. The decorator rushed to the farmhouse to raise the alarm, where he was met with the horrid scene of John James Blackburn lying dead on the floor with a gun at his side. After committing his gruesome deeds, Blackburn had turned the gun on himself. The decorator rushed to the village, but Foulds Wilkinson had already given the alarm. He had returned earlier, and, having seen the carnage, had informed the police at Burnley. The scenes of slaughter were not yet over, for as they inspected the shippon, they found the body of the cowman Joseph Henry Scriven – he too had been shot. On a window ledge nearby, a note was found written in Blackburn's hand, it read: 'Well, Foulds, I thought this would punish you more than anything else. I am not crazy, but just getting my own back. I leave you to look after my brother.' All the victims of what became known as 'The Worsthorne Massacre' were buried in the village on the same day, 6 February 1937.

1852   Robert Brindle, an overseer at Morris's factory in Oldfield Road, Salford was brought to Salford Town Hall and charged with a serious assault upon Mary Larkin, a mill operative at the factory. Larkin stated that she approached Brindle to defend a little boy from a charge of using ill language, which two other workers had complained about. A heated exchange of words followed and Brindle then knocked Larkin to the floor and held her down by her hair – this caused a considerable amount of hair loss. For a number of minutes she was also insensible. The defendant did not deny the assault, but stated that the complainant frequently caused disorder in the factory, and on this occasion was asked repeatedly to be quiet before he was obliged to put her out. The magistrates said that no matter what the conduct had been, the defendant had no right to resort to such violence, and bound him over to the sum of £5 to keep the peace for six months.   **28 JANUARY**

1789   The parish records for the beautiful church of Newchurch-in-Pendle, near the foot of Pendle Hill, Lancashire has the following entry: **29 JANUARY**

On the 29th of this month [January 1789] was interred at Newchurch-in-Pendle the body of Hannah Corbridge, of this chapelry, concerning whom the following narrative deserves to be recorded. She went on Sunday afternoon, the 19th instant, from her father's house at Narrs, with her lover Christopher Hartley of Barnside, a young man aged 19 years of age. She was never seen afterwards till next Sunday afternoon, when she was found in a ditch near home, poisoned and having her throat cut. On the next Sunday forenoon the murderer was brought back to Colne, having been apprehended at Flookborough, was found guilty by Coroner's Jury, committed to Lancaster Castle, convicted and executed on 28th August.

Narrs, Hannah's home – and Barnside, for that matter – still exists on the A6068 between Colne and Keighley, and just beyond Laneshaw Bridge, towards Yorkshire. Legend says that the spirit of poor Hannah Corbridge used to wander around Narrs and Barnside for many years after she was murdered, until she was 'layed' by a local Catholic priest. The Barnside we see today has been rebuilt. When the old building was pulled down, the stone was reused at Laneshaw Bridge. Here, according to local tradition, the stones turned blood-red and 'wept' on each anniversary of Hannah Corbridge's death.

Narrs, a lonely farmhouse on the hills above Laneshaw Bridge – the home of Hannah Corbridge, who was murdered by her lover. (Jack Nadin)

30 JANUARY 1865 Irishman Stephen Burke, well known to the police, was arrested on a charge of murdering his wife. Burke resided at 51 Brunswick Street, Preston, and, in the early hours of the morning, screams were heard by the other neighbours – but the noises did not raise any particular attention, as they were frequently heard coming from the house. However, this time the quietness that followed did arouse suspicion, and the police were called to the house at around 9 o'clock in the morning. The wife had been dead for some time. The weapon appeared to have been a bedpost about 4in thick – it still bore the marks of clotted blood. The

pair had been married for around fourteen years and had five children, the eldest little more than 12 years old, the youngest a child in arms. The eldest daughter, Mary Ann Burke, later gave evidence. She said:

I am the daughter of the prisoner, I am a little over 12 years of age. My father came home yesterday about 4 o'clock – he was in liquor and was aggressive. My mother went to bed around 10 o'clock, as did I and all the other children. I slept at the foot of the bed where my mother was, father went to bed afterwards. About 4 o'clock father went into another room, and came back with a bedpost in his hand with which he struck my mother twice about the head. My mother moaned and complained, I got up and went for the light. I went out of the house and did not return – I stayed in a lobby all night.

The girl was getting very upset at this stage, and was asked to step down. Police Constable Clarkson stated:

When I went to the house occupied by the prisoner, the door was fast. I burst the door open, I saw the prisoner on the stairs. I asked him what the cause of the row was this morning. He said 'Nothing'. I went upstairs and saw the deceased on the bed. I felt the body of the deceased and it was quite cold.

Burke was executed at Lancaster Castle on 25 March 1865; it was the last public hanging to take place there.

31 JANUARY

1841 Two of the workmen employed at the Oldham Gas Works at Lee's Brook, Oldham went down into a 15ft-deep well in order to remedy a defect. One of them, Samuel Taylor, took out a plug, and, in doing so, gas rushed into the well – they instantly suffocated. The alarm was given by Taylor's wife, and several people rushed to the spot. After much difficulty, the bodies were retrieved from the well. Mr James Lawton, a surgeon, was in attendance within a few minutes, and resorted to the best method of restoring animation – that of bleeding the jugular vein and arm, inflating the lungs, and placing the men in a warm bath. After these efforts, Kay was brought back to life, but Taylor was past recovery. Taylor was the superintendent of the works, and left a wife and two children to mourn his loss.

FEBRUARY

Manchester Assizes, where Robert Beswick stood trial for wounding James Roscoe.
(*See* 17 February.)

1 FEBRUARY   **1879**   Mary Cash, aged 15, worked as a domestic for Miss Mary Ann Staniforth, an aging milliner. On this night, the servant girl was sent to the cellar for some beer. When she came back, the old woman noticed that the beer was 'muddy', and she asked the servant girl if she had shaken the barrel, to which the girl replied 'No'. Miss Staniforth drank some of the ale and immediately became seriously ill. Dr Lancashire was sent for, and, on analysing the remains of the beer in the glass, he concluded that there appeared to be about a spoonful of red precipitate, sufficient to endanger the life of Miss Staniforth, present in the liquid. It was later shown that a quantity of this powder had been sent to Mary Cash by her parents, who lived at Willenhall in Coventry. In her defence it was stated that she had put some of the precipitate on her hair, which could have fallen out as she was pouring the beer from the barrel. However, it appeared that the girl had been in trouble a number of times before, and consequently she was committed for trial on a charge of attempted murder.

2 FEBRUARY

The scene of a fearful accident at Bury, when the floor of a building collapsed.

1874   A terrible accident occurred at Bury whereby nine lives were lost and over thirty people were injured when the floor of a building gave way. The accident happened on the upper floor of a quilting warehouse on Paradise Street, occupied by Messrs Butcher and Chadwick, in a room being used as a meeting place for a Liberal campaign. It appeared that originally there were pillars installed to support the floors, but these had been removed so that the operatives had more room to work. The meeting was called by the principal Liberal, Mr Philips, and word soon got round – mainly amongst the Irish Catholics, who started to gather around the building. Soon there was pushing and shoving as the crowd tried to get into the room itself, when suddenly a portion of the floor (27ft by 20ft) gave way under the weight. A mass of human beings fell 30ft to the ground floor; screams echoed and cries rang out as broken bodies fell among shattered timbers, soot and dust. Mr Philips and his supporters were completely cut off, as the portion of the floor where they had been sitting remained intact. Help was soon at hand but it took a number of hours to get the dead and injured out of the wrecked building – almost all of the dead being Roman Catholics. An inquest held later returned a verdict of 'accidental death' in all cases, and all parties concerned were exonerated from blame.

1846   An inquest was held at the Red Lion Inn, Quarlton on the body of 8-year-old Ralph Scholes, who drowned in a coal pit. It appeared that the deceased and thirteen others had been working in the pit at Quarlton when one of the men struck into an old mine, which had been standing for thirty-six years. The water rushed in on them and they were driven forward to the pit shaft. The men assisted in getting the boys out, and all were rescued apart from Ralph. A verdict of 'accidental death' was recorded.

3 FEBRUARY

1833   Child cruelty is despicable, and when a child dies at the hands of those who should be caring for him or her, it raises even greater anger – such was the case in Rochdale in 1833. Ann Jane Hindley was the illegitimate child of John Leigh and his wife, and was aged just 3 when her drunken father savagely beat her with his fists because she would not give him an embrace. The child's wounds included bleeding around the brain, massive bruising around the stomach, and discolouration around the head, face and belly. The poor child was quickly removed to her maternal grandmother's house, where she cried out pitifully and repeatedly, 'Daddy has killed me! Daddy has killed me!' She died on 4 February, and the jury at the inquest recorded a verdict of manslaughter against the father – but he, probably knowing the outcome, had absconded. A warrant was issued for his apprehension – but whether he was caught or not does not appear to have been recorded.

4 FEBRUARY

1875   A fatal fire broke out at the Spinners Arms, kept by Henry Astley at Bamber Bridge near Preston. Early in the morning, the landlord was awakened by a loud crackling sound and, on opening his bedroom door, he was immediately forced back by the volume of smoke. He went to his wife and told her to follow him; they broke a window and made their escape. However, several other people remained in the house – one of them, a lady named Mrs Dewhurst, rushed out through the

5 FEBRUARY

same window and was saved. In the upper storey there were three men and a boy named William Waring. One of the men jumped through a window and another got onto a roof, whilst the third groped his way downstairs. One of these men, George Sim, then went back upstairs for the lad, but could not find him. Further attempts were made to find the boy, and on the third he was found on a landing, scorched and burnt – he was dead. The fire was eventually put out by means of buckets, and the cause was thought to have been some clothes hanging near a fire to dry.

6 FEBRUARY **1874** A fire broke out at the warehouse of H. Tate & Son, sugar refiners at Liverpool, which in spite of the efforts of the firemen was not extinguished until the building was gutted. A fireman named Burgess was knocked off a ladder by a coping stone and died.

7 FEBRUARY **1821** As Mr Birchall, of the Clerks of the Peace Office in Preston, and Mr Chaffer of Burnley, Bridgemaster, were returning from Tarleton in a gig, they were attacked near Preston by five highwaymen. One of the men called upon them to stop, and three of the gang (armed with pistols) left the footpath and approached the gig. Mr Chaffer, who held the reigns, was preparing to strike a blow with his whip, but Mr Birchall urged him to push on, which he accordingly did, and thus they escaped. One of the villains, however, did fire a pistol at them.

8 FEBRUARY **1852** Mr E. Herford, the borough coroner, held an inquest at Yorkshire House in Pin Mill Brow, Ardwick, on the body of Richard Leonard, a 34-year-old bricklayer's labourer. For some time the deceased had had no regular abode and had been in the habit of sleeping in the lime kilns at the Ardwick Lane Lime Works. On the previous Sunday, one of the men employed at the works had looked into a kiln where some lime was burning and found in it the dead body of Leonard. The head and one of the arms were burned off. It was shown at the inquest that the deceased had been in a state of intoxication the night before, and it was therefore assumed that he had gone, as usual, to his lime to sleep but had lost his footing and fallen in. The jury returned a verdict of 'accidental death'.

9 FEBRUARY **1886** Fish merchant John Baines, aged 41, of Barrow-in-Furness and his wife, Ellen, were constantly arguing – he had threatened to take her life many times, but she had simply stopped taking notice. Just before Christmas 1885, Baines once again uttered, 'One of these days I'm going to kill thee lass.' The threats and arguments continued throughout Christmas Day and, eventually, Ellen had taken all the abuse she could;

she packed her bags and moved into a neighbour's house. Baines was furious; he picked up a butcher's knife and went round to the neighbour's house, banging loudly on the front door. Eventually Ellen opened the door, and John Baines plunged the knife into her body. Not content with that, he withdrew the knife and stuck it back into Ellen another three times. The horrified neighbour looked on, and, as Baines turned to walk away, he said, 'If she isn't dead now, she ought to be.' Baines was quickly apprehended, and at his trial a month later, his solicitor stated that he 'was under the disillusionment that his wife was being unfaithful to him', and put forward plea of insanity. The jury dismissed this plea and found Baines guilty, and on Tuesday, 9 February 1886, he was hanged at Lancaster Prison for his crime.

1851 Horatio Nelson Harrison was brought before the borough court   10 FEBRUARY
at Oldham to answer a charge of ill-treating his wife. At about half past eight the previous Saturday evening, a woman ran into the office at Oldham Road police station, closely followed by the prisoner, whom she accused of having ill-treated her in a shameless manner. The woman told the officer to look in the prisoner's pockets and, on doing so, the officer found a weapon of a most murderous description. It consisted of a piece of wood about 6in long and 3in in circumference, with a loop of thick, twisted cord at one end which could be passed over the wrist. A piece of cord, about 6in in length, was fastened to the other end of the handle, to which a ball of lead weighing 2lbs was attached. It would appear almost impossible for a person who received a blow from such a weapon to survive. The prisoner stated in his defence that he was obliged to carry the weapon in order to defend himself from the men who followed his wife, and who were always looking out for a chance to thrash him. There were many policemen who knew that his wife was as bad as any in England. It was stated that when the complainant was examined at the station, her legs, thighs and several other parts of her body were much bruised – she, however, failed to turn up at the hearing and the defendant was discharged. When told that the weapon would not be returned to him, the prisoner replied, 'Then if I am not to have that, I shall have to carry a pistol, for I must defend myself.'

1850 A fatal accident occurred at Cliviger near Burnley. A 22-year-   11 FEBRUARY
old railway worker, William Burrows, was filling a wagon with earth – which had fallen from the side of a cutting around 12-14ft deep – when an enormous earth slide took place. Seeing this, Burrows leaped out of the way, but fell with his back against the wagon; the earth buried his lower half. When extricated a short time afterwards, he complained of pains in his stomach and lower legs. He was attended to by a surgeon,

who was with him until his death a few hours later. The inquest was held at the Ram Inn in the village.

12 FEBRUARY 1853 An inquest was held at the Scarisbrick Arms, Halsall on the death of 42-year-old Thomas Ball. The deceased had returned from Ormskirk on 1 February in the company of another man, and, when they had reached Lamancha Lodge, his companion had exited the carriage to open the gate, when the belly band on his horse snapped and Ball was thrown out. Several of his ribs were broken and he was injured about the head. He lingered until Monday, when he finally expired.

13 FEBRUARY 1852 James Walsh, a weaver, was injured in rather a strange way as he left the Grey Horse Inn at Darwen. He was leaving by the back door, where some people were engaged in rifle practice in the yard, when a ball rebounded off the iron target and struck Walsh on the left temple, causing a laceration on his face down to his ear. Luckily a surgeon was soon on the spot and Walsh was said to have been in a favourable state.

14 FEBRUARY 1850 An inquest was held at Clayton-le-Moors on the body of 52-year-old Robert Calvert. The deceased was a steamer in a calico printing works. On 2 January, he left home with his son and went to a local beer shop where they drank until two o'clock in the afternoon. The deceased then went to several other beerhouses and ended up at an alehouse in Church. At the end of the day, he and several others were making their way up Dill Hall Lane, when halfway up he stopped and urged the others to carry on. That was the last time he was ever seen alive; he was later found floating in the Leeds & Liverpool Canal, dead.

15 FEBRUARY 1887 Katherine Quinn, aged 40, was a habitual drunk, as was her husband. After a violent argument, she left him and moved in with another drunk, 47-year-old Thomas Leatherbarrow, at his home in Pendleton, Salford. Katherine was hoping for a little rest from the drink and the argumentative life she had been living, but it was not to be. Both Katherine and Leatherbarrow were in a state of intoxication on New Year's Eve 1886, when he threatened to kill her – not for the first time. She survived, and on another drinking session on Saturday, 8 January 1887, he carried out his threat by brutally kicking her to death. He then callously left her and simply carried on with his drinking. He was soon arrested, and in reply to questions by the police, said, 'I finished her off wi' mi' clogs.' He pleaded guilty at his trial, and was found likewise and hanged at Strangeways Prison, Manchester on 15 February 1887.

1889 A catastrophe was reported upon. The disaster occurred on 8 February at Little Lever near Bolton, whereby seven people lost their lives when some cottages were destroyed. The two cottages formed a court in a row of houses off High Street, and were overshadowed by a factory erected by a Mr Hulme of Radcliffe about thirty years previous. For many years the mill had been unoccupied, and on one side all of the windows had been broken. It was conjectured that the strong winds on that day had entered through the open windows and into the enclosed space of the mill, forcing the walls outwards. The gable end of the factory fell upon the cottages, the weight of the bricks and stones crushing the roofs and bedrooms and throwing the front walls across to some cottages close by. The debris was strewn everywhere; furniture, bedclothes and broken glass, along with broken bodies, littered the front of the old houses. There were thirteen people in the houses before the disaster struck – all in the lower rooms – happily seven of these escaped. In Mrs Riley's house there was, besides herself, her daughter Elizabeth, aged 19, James Riley, aged 7, and Sarah Ann Riley, aged 5. The three children were found dead amongst the debris. In another house, occupied by a widow named Pendlebury, another three lives were lost – herself, her daughter and her granddaughter. A 2-year-old child was found under the rubble, badly burned; the falling bricks had forced him against an open fire. Accidental death was returned in all the cases.

Rescuers grapple through the fallen debris after a disaster at Little Lever.

1874 Fifteen-year-old James Roscoe worked at Hardcastle & Co.'s bleach-works at Firwood near Bolton, and was on his way to his employment at around 6 a.m. As he passed a place known as 'The Nook', he saw Robert Beswick, a youth slightly older than himself, who called out, 'Come here, I want thee.' Not recognising at the time just who he was, James ran off, but Beswick chased after him. Drawing something out of his pocket, Beswick threw Roscoe to the ground and cut his throat. A struggle followed and Roscoe was able to escape, but as he ran away Beswick called out that he would put a rag on his throat. The injured lad carried on running until he arrived at the bleach-works – his throat bleeding all the way. He was taken home and attended to by Dr Smith, who found a gaping wound, 1.5in across and about a quarter of an inch deep. Robert Beswick was arrested by PC Bradbury the following day, and when charged, replied, 'I thought I was using the back of the knife, I did not intend to cut, I only wanted to frighten him.' At the magistrates' court, Beswick was committed to the Manchester Assizes on a charge of 'cutting and wounding with intent to do grievous bodily harm'.

18 FEBRUARY 1854   The *Preston Guardian* reported:

> On the night of Saturday the 4th inst., the constable of Skerton was taking his rounds when his attention was called to a noise coming from a house of a man named Wilson. Looking through a hole which had been made in a window shutter, he saw two cocks fighting on the floor and about a score of men and boys congregated to witness the fight. Wilson was summoned before the magistrates at the Judges Lodgings on Saturday last for permitting cockfighting at his house. The charge was proved and Wilson was fined 5 shillings and 14 shillings costs.

19 FEBRUARY 1841   Around 6.30 p.m., as Mrs Mann and Mr Harrison were returning from Melton near Manchester, they were stopped by five footpads, pulled off their horses and robbed. The thieves took from Mr Harrison £100 in Leicester bank notes, about eight sovereigns, 28s in silver, and a gold watch. Mr Mann was relieved of £55.

20 FEBRUARY 1831   A young courting couple were out walking by the reservoir near the Bolton cotton mill belonging to Ormerod & Hardcastle, when the girl noticed a floating bundle. The lad dragged the bundle to the side and, opening it up, both were horrified to uncover the dead body of an infant girl. The inquest was held at the Three Arrows, which established that the child had been born alive, but she showed signs of a violent blow to the skull. With little other evidence to go on, the inquest returned a verdict of 'wilful murder by person or persons unknown'. A short time later, a 24-year-old lass, Charlotte Gray of Middle Street in Bolton, was arrested. She was known to have been heavily pregnant a short while before, but there was no sign of the baby. When questioned, she said that she had given birth to a still-born child, but was so upset that she threw it out of the window! It was not possible to prove that Charlotte had killed the child, but nevertheless she was charged with the lesser crime of concealing a birth and found guilty. She was sentenced to two years' imprisonment at Lancaster Castle – the judge stated that in his opinion she was guilty of a much higher crime. The little human being was buried all alone in a pauper's grave, unloved and uncared for in its short life. She was not even given the dignity of having a name.

1848   At a meeting of the Poor Law Board of Guardians at Blackburn, the chairman drew attention to a placard in town which had appeared on the previous Thursday. It alleged that a woman named Ellen Davies, whose husband was receiving outdoor relief, had died from starvation. The placard also contained a serious charge against Mr Ashton, the relieving officer, of having used violent language against the husband when he applied for extra relief preceding his wife's death. From the books it appeared that her family had been in regular weekly receipt of 5s, and that 6s 6d had been given to them the week before her death.

21 FEBRUARY

1876   At about eight o'clock in the morning, a letter carrier for the Colne district found the body of a man half-buried in the snow on a footpath close to the highway near Trawden Cemetery. The deceased was William Blackburn, a 60-year-old labourer. It appeared that he had left home in good health the previous night and was seen during the day at Colne. About six o'clock on the same night he was seen drunk on a footpath near Carry Bridge. He stumbled and a lady assisted him; he continued his journey towards home, but must have died during the night.

22 FEBRUARY

1855   County coroner, Mr Driffield, held an inquest at the Angel Inn, Ashton-in-Makerfield on the death of an unidentified man who had died in a common lodging house from taking two pennyworth of opium, which he had purchased at a druggist shop shortly after taking lodgings at the house. The jury returned a verdict in accordance with the circumstances.

23 FEBRUARY

1844   About ten o'clock on the previous Wednesday morning, 60-year-old James Hargreaves from Freetown, Bury died after eating some porridge which was mixed with arsenic. It appeared that the old man had mistakenly taken the poison from a shelf, and, along with his grandson, a boy aged 4, had eaten it by mistake. The old man died, but with the aid of medical assistance the lad was saved and made a full recovery.

24 FEBRUARY

1854   The cotton factory belonging to William Warburton at Gigg, near Bury, was discovered to be on fire. So rapid was the progress of the flames, that twenty minutes after it started the roof fell in with a tremendous crash and the whole premises was reduced to a pile of rubble. The mill was an old building, the property of Mr Grundy of Park Hills, and, as the floors were saturated with oil, the flames ascended to a great altitude. Four engines were brought to the spot. When the engines

25 FEBRUARY

arrived, however, the factory was completely gutted, and the intention of the firemen was to try and save the adjoining property. The mill was four storeys plus an attic; the length of the building was 150ft and the breadth 42ft. The damage was estimated at between £7,000 and £8,000. Thousands of people visited the scene of the fire the following day.

26 FEBRUARY **1847** An inquest was held at the Commercial Inn at Church near Oswaldtwistle on the death of 41-year-old James Bury. The deceased was a block cutter who grew depressed from the lack of trade. He had lived in Manchester but decided that the country air might agree with him more and moved to Church. However, he grew worse. On Monday he got up early; his sister heard him rise and also got up. As she was dressing, she heard a moan coming from the cellar. On investigation she found the deceased lying on his back, his throat cut and the jugular vein and windpipe severed – there was a great amount of blood; he was dead. The verdict of the jury was that he destroyed himself in a fit of insanity.

27 FEBRUARY **1854** John Hoyle, a tailor from Tottington Lower End, was descending some steps leading from a beerhouse at Ramsbottom, when he fell down the stairs and died within five minutes. He had been drinking for several days.

28 FEBRUARY **1857** Ann Coates, wife of blacksmith John Coates, was at the courthouse due to the following circumstances: On Saturday morning, someone entered the house of John Turner, weaver of Brunshaw Road, Burnley, after he and his wife had gone to work. The trespasser opened the drawer of the dresser and took a black silk petticoat, a blue petticoat, four yards of new flannelling, two pieces of sheeting, two night jackets and other articles of clothing. Turner and his wife had left the back door open so that Mrs Turner's young sister could fetch a little girl who was left in bed. The sister went for the girl at about seven o'clock and found the back door wide open and all of the dresser drawers open. Turner and his wife were sent for. On Saturday night, the black silk petticoat was found at Mr Catton's pawnbrokers on Hammerton Street. Mrs Turner identified the property as her own, and the pawnbroker said that they were pledged by Ann Coates. Mrs Turner said that she did not think the prisoner had taken the articles, as she suspected someone else. Mr Baldwin, who appeared for the prisoner, pressed Mrs Turner to name the suspected person, but she declined. Witnesses who lived with the prisoner were called on her behalf, and stated that the prisoner was ill on the night in question and neither they nor her had been out of the house.

The magistrates dismissed the case on her husband, who entered into his own recognisances to produce his wife if called upon the charge within three months.

MARCH

The Edisford Bridge Hotel, where John Dawson spent his last night drinking before being murdered.
(*See* 19 March.)

1 MARCH   1884   A sad affair occurred at Chadderton Town Hall. Entertainment was being put on for the children of members of the local Co-operative Society. Mr Diggle was putting on a magic lantern exhibition, and for the purpose of illumination he was using oxygen light. A reservoir of the gas was placed in front of the stage. The hall was eventually crowded with children aged from 6-12 years. Suddenly, there was an unusually quick expansion of the oxygen bag, which was followed by a terrific explosion. The windows were shattered and the gas lights were blown out in the hall. The children panicked and ran for the doors, and happily most made their escape unharmed. However, one little chap, 6-year-old William Heywood, was found dead on a staircase, and nearly a dozen or so other children were injured to some extent. The damage to the hall amounted to around £100, and the event caused great excitement in and around Chadderton. It was after midnight before the crowds dispersed.

The scene at Chadderton Town Hall, where an explosion occurred.

2 MARCH   1867   There was a terrible fire at Accrington which claimed the lives of nine young children. The fire broke out at the heald knitting place, occupied by James Duckworth, under the railway arches of the Lancashire & Yorkshire Railway that runs through the centre of town, and near to the Black Bull Inn. The works occupied the whole of the ground floor, but the second floor was used as a Catholic school, and at the time of the blaze there was upwards of 100 children in the place. Many of the children were able to escape before the fire brought down the stairways, whilst others ran to the windows and were rescued by ladder – nine of them, however, perished in the flames. The little ones who died that sad day were: 6-year-old Mary Alice Duckworth, daughter of James Duckworth; 6-year-old Elizabeth Jane Wade; 6-year-old Mary Bentley; 5-year-old Catherine Lantey; 4-year-old Ellen Ann Varley; 4-year-old Robert Land; 4-year-old Mary Ann Fish; 5-year-old Elizabeth Proctor; and 3-year-old Thomas Jackson. An inquest was later held at the Crown Hotel, Accrington, where the verdict was that 'The children

The fire at Accrington in which nine children died on 2 March 1867.

had been burnt to death but by what means the fire was started there was no evidence to show'.

1846   An inquest was held at the Bowling Green Inn, Ashton-under-Lyne, on the body of a young child found floating in the Ashton Canal the previous Sunday. The surgeon revealed that the child was dead before entering the canal, and had been horribly mutilated. The cause of death

3 MARCH

The Bowling Green Inn, where the inquest was held on an unnamed infant found horribly murdered in the Ashton Canal.

was a skull fracture, whereby a portion of the bone had been driven into the brain. There was also a fracture of the arm, between the shoulder and elbow, and there was another wound in the groin, 4in in length, extending into the abdomen through which the bowels protruded. All of the wounds appeared to have been made by a sharp instrument – the surgeon thought that the child had only lived a few hours. The jury returned a verdict of 'wilful murder against some person at present unknown'. The police, it was stated, were 'sparing no pains to find the unnatural mother'.

4 MARCH **1847** John Howcroft was brought before the borough court at Bolton on a charge of pulling out the tongue of a horse. The horse was the property of Charles Nuttall of Bolton. John Duckworth, the carter, was driving the horse up Crown Street when the animal became restless. Howcroft stepped in and said he knew how to make it move. With that, he got hold of the horse's tongue and pulled until he nearly drew it out of its mouth. The result was that the poor animal had to be destroyed. It was stated that the horse was old, and not of much value. Howcroft agreed to pay £2 and expenses, and on that condition the case was dismissed.

5 MARCH **1848** John Harrison, aged 19, was an apprentice to a clogger. He was brought up before the Bench, along with Nancy Morris, aged 30, and was charged with causing a false entry in the register of marriages at Prestwich church. The woman was also charged with having two husbands. The prisoners were married at Prestwich on 16 January and presented themselves both of age, although Harrison was only 19. They also stated that they belonged to Prestwich, although they were actually living in Farnworth. The offence was felony, rendering them liable on conviction to transportation, and not less than two years' imprisonment. Nancy Morris was first married about eleven years earlier, but her husband was afterwards transported, and, as it could not be proved whether or not he was alive at the time of the second marriage, the charge of bigamy was abandoned. The prisoners were then committed for trial for causing a false entry in the parish register at Prestwich.

6 MARCH **1831** Christopher Wilcock, a simple-looking farmer, was charged with having forged two promissory notes for the payment of £76 each, with intent to defraud his landlord John Wilson Patten, MP at Winmarleigh near Garstang. Evidence was heard that established the guilt of the prisoner, and the death penalty was passed against him.

1544 This was the year of the building of the 'new' church in Newchurch-in-Pendle in the east of Lancashire. This beautiful little village, with its whitewashed cottages, clings to the hillside near Pendle Hill, which is famed for the Pendle Witches, or Lancashire Witches as they are sometimes known. The church tower itself has a feature known as the 'Eye of God', said to protect the village from evil – but in all probability it is just a walled-up window. Near the entrance to the church, on the right-hand side of the doorway, is a supposed witch's grave – actually just a grave to one of the Nutter family, a common name in this area. But there was, of course, a Lancashire witch named Alice Nutter. However, a witch would never be buried in consecrated ground. It is still possible to see an old horseshoe nailed to some of the old cottage doors here; this was another form of protection from the witches, as was any stone with a hole in it. Tales of the old witches are revived at the famous Witches Galore gift shop, just up the road from the church. This has a good collection of books, broomsticks and other witch memorabilia.

7 MARCH

1842 In the early hours of the morning, two policemen on duty on the Ashton Road at Ardwick heard a moan coming from behind some brick kilns. Searching, they found a man on his back in a pit of water about 25 yards from Ashton New Road, and about 20 yards from Bank Meadow Street. When the man was pulled out he was quite insensible, but did show signs of recovery. He was taken to the surgeon, Mr Boyers of Pin Mill Brow, where restoratives were put to use, but to no avail. It later emerged that the man was named John Cliffe, and worked as a fustian shearer. He had been drinking that night in the alehouses around Ancoats Street with a companion named Mills, but they had parted company around 9.45 p.m. At the inquest, it was stated that he was addicted to alcohol, and it was supposed that while in a state of intoxication he had fallen into the pit and was unable to extricate himself. A verdict to that effect was returned.

8 MARCH

1871 At the Stake Pool Station on the Knott End to Garstang line, an accident occurred by which a local farmer was fatally injured. Ralph Mason was there with his horse and cart on some business, when the horse got restive and ran the cart against a wagon. Mason was caught in between – he died almost instantly.

9 MARCH

1537 On this day, Abbot John Paslew, who was born in the nearby village of Wiswell and for thirty years was in charge of Whalley Abbey, was hanged at Lancaster Castle for not swearing to the Oath of Allegiance. Local tradition conflicts with the records of his death, and states that he was hanged at the monastery gates and buried in the churchyard at Whalley.

10 MARCH

A view of Whalley Abbey from the other side of the river Calder, where John Paslew was the last abbot. (Taken from *The History of Whalley*)

Within the churchyard there is a gravestone, said by some to be the tomb of Abbot John, the last abbot at Whalley, who died for his faith.

11 MARCH   1902   Mary Crompton was a pretty young lass from Bolton, who by the age of 22 found herself in the family way. Times proved hard for a young girl in Mary's situation – there was no welfare service in those days – but she did manage to get a job as a domestic servant at the Victoria Hotel in Westhoughton. She also arranged to have her child looked after by a lady named Ellen Lee, who lived on the Bolton Road in Westhoughton, and Mary visited the child on a regular basis. On 11 March 1902, when the child was about 7 months old, Mary Crompton came to the Lees' household and announced that she would be taking the child to visit a Mr Potter. The mother returned at about 9.30 p.m., and Ellen noticed that there was something seriously wrong with the child. The baby was frothing at the mouth, which was swollen and blistered, and crying out in pain. When asked by Ellen if she had given anything to the child, Mary appeared confused and simply blurted out that she had only given it 'some thick Spanish'. There was a strong smell of carbolic, and Ellen removed the baby's frock which was saturated with it. The mother appeared even more confused, and turned around and simply left the house. The child was eventually taken to a doctor, who stated that someone had tried to feed the baby carbolic acid. Fortunately, not enough had been consumed to cause any serious harm to the child. There was enough concern for the police to become involved, and the mother was arrested and taken to the local police station. When questioned, she told the officers that

The Victoria Hotel.

life as a single mother was all too much for her, and she had decided to 'make away with the child' and herself. She had found the carbolic in a cupboard at the Victoria Hotel, and had given it to her baby. She was committed for trial at the Manchester Assizes on a charge of murder – the law would take its course and Mary Crompton would never again see her child.

1836 Joseph Watson was a tailor and draper at Bradshawgate near Bolton. He was a single man who lived by himself, although he kept an apprentice to look after the shop while he was away. On 12 March 1836, Watson was in his shop with the apprentice when a friend of his, John Kearney, came in. Kearney asked Watson if he had had breakfast, but received no reply. Just then, Watson pulled a pistol out of his pocket and was about to place it in his mouth when the apprentice wrestled it off him. He then pulled out another pistol, which Kearney managed to get off him. Watson then rushed upstairs to his bedroom, followed by Kearney, and, after a struggle, Kearney managed to calm him down and secure the bedroom door before going for help. Kearney returned to the house again, just as there was another gunshot. He found Watson 'lying on the floor weltering in his blood'. He had destroyed himself by placing a gun in his mouth. It was reported that: 'The contents [of the shot] came out at the back of his head, parts of the skull and brain adhering to the ceiling of the room.' Some papers were found later which indicated that Watson was in financial difficulties. A verdict of 'destroyed himself in a fit of temporary insanity' was later recorded at an inquest.

12 MARCH

13 MARCH 1865 Considerable excitement prevailed in Bacup following a report that a child had been found in a meadow at Moss Gap with its throat cut. At about 9.30 a.m., a man was walking through a meadow with the Bacup beagles when he observed a parcel behind a wall. Upon examination, it was found that the parcel contained the lifeless body of a fully grown female child. The man passed the information on to the police at once, and a medical man expressed the opinion that the child had been placed where it was found soon after birth, but he could not say whether it had been born alive or not. He found wounds upon the right shoulder, under the right ear, and on the face. The police were of the opinion that the body had been attacked either by rats or dogs, as the wrapper was open and the wounds described above exposed.

14 MARCH 1857 A severe gale force wind was raging in and around Bolton, near Hugh Jones's brickworks in Willows. Sixteen-year-old William Hutchinson was going about his duties when a sudden gust blew down a brick shed. One of the walls fell onto William, killing him instantly. Another man working in a clay-hole close by escaped without injury, and, remarkably, four men at work inside the shed also escaped unscathed. The piles of bricks in the yard outside had protected them from the falling debris and the timbers as the roof crashed in.

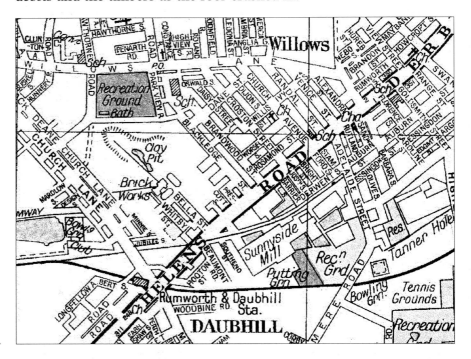

The brickworks where William Hutchinson was killed in a freak accident has now gone, but shows up on this 1930s' map.

15 MARCH 1855 An inquest was held at the Duke of York public house, Regent Road, on the body of Joseph Capon, a Private in the King's Own Light

Infantry, who committed suicide in the hospital of Regent Road Barracks by cutting his throat with a razor. The deceased was aged 36 and had been attached to the regiment for seventeen years. On the previous Wednesday, he had complained of a pain in the left side of his chest, and was sent to the barracks hospital. The deceased had been drinking for several days beforehand and was addicted to liquor – but he was respectable, his father being connected with the Bank of England. Anthony Mealey, a patient on the same ward, stated that he had heard Capon breathing heavily, and when he approached his bed he found Capon's throat cut and a razor in his right hand. Henry Laine, the assistant hospital surgeon, stated that he had talked to Capon five minutes before his death, and he had showed symptoms of brain fever. Every soldier was allowed a razor when in hospital, and they kept it beside their bed. A verdict was returned to the effect that the deceased had committed suicide during temporary insanity.

1857 At the courthouse, Thomas Hodgeon of Burnley Lane, Burnley was charged with stealing a quantity of props and planks from a culvert under the embankment of the East Lancashire Railway near Barden. The 160-yard long culvert was propped for about 100 yards in the centre, with planks and stays across. On examination, it was found that all of the props had been taken down, and parts carried away; some parts were lying in the bottom of the culvert. What had been removed was worth about £10 or £12. Several courses of stone had given way on the removal of the props. Some of the planks had been found in the garden of a mechanic, John Rawlinson, who stated that he had bought them from a man named Richard Barcroft. The timber was branded 'R & W.H', for Messrs R. & W. Hattersley. When the prisoner was apprehended he denied having sold any timber to Rawlinson – but he was committed for trial. 16 MARCH

1883 An extraordinary incident took place near Ince Station, Wigan resulting in the death of one man, and several narrow escapes. Without any warning, the fronts of two cottages in Viaduct Street gave way, and disappeared in a loud crash down an old coal shaft, which suddenly disclosed itself. A man named John Bankes, who was passing one of the doors at that moment, was engulfed with the falling debris, and his body has never been recovered. His wife, who was nearly blind, narrowly escaped. The accident caused great consternation and other houses in the neighbourhood were vacated by tenants. 17 MARCH

1612 John Law, a pedlar, was selling his wares in Colne Field, near Colne, when he was cursed by a beggar girl named Alizon Device for refusing to give her some pins. Moments later, he collapsed with paralysis of the limbs (most likely he suffered from a stroke). Alizon Device, however, was 18 MARCH

Hanging the Lancashire Witches at Lancaster Castle.

convinced she was the cause and confessed to bewitching him. In court, she confessed her family's involvement with witchcraft in great detail. Things moved quickly, and, on 2 April 1612, Demdike, Anne Chattox and Anne Redferne were interrogated about their involvement in witchcraft at Ashlar House. On 27 April, Elizabeth, James and Jennet Device were also questioned at Ashlar House. From such humble beginnings began what has been described by some as one of the greatest miscarriages of justice in British history. The trial of the Pendle Witches took place at Lancaster on Monday, 17 August 1612. This resulted in the hanging at Lancaster Prison, on 20 August, of Alizon Device, Elizabeth Device, James Device, Anne Redferne, Alice Nutter, Katherine Hewitt, John Bulcock, Jane Bulcock, Isobel Robey and Anne Chattox – only one accused 'witch' was found to be not guilty. All of these 'witches' were executed because of the ignorance and fears of the times. The Padiham witch, Margaret Pearson, was also arrested in 1612 by the local constable. Pearson was charged with bewitching a horse, and was taken to Lancaster Castle to stand trial along with the so-called 'notorious witches of Pendle'. She, though, was spared death and sentenced to be pilloried on four successive market days at Padiham, Clitheroe, Whalley and Lancaster before commencing a year in jail.

19 MARCH **1934** John Dawson lived with his sisters, Annie, Lily and Polly, at Bashall Eves on the outskirts of Clitheroe. It was a wild March night when 46-year-old Dawson left the comfortable surroundings of the Edisford Bridge Hotel a few minutes before nine o'clock in the evening. Dawson put his head down against the strong wind as he began his twenty-

minute walk back home. About halfway home he was near-blinded by the headlights of an oncoming car – but he noticed that one of the occupants of the car was a man by the name of Tom Kenyon, one of his hired help. Dawson had earlier asked Kenyon if he cared to come for a drink with him – Kenyon had replied in the negative, and it seems that Kenyon was then off to the better night life in nearby Clitheroe. As Dawson passed the entrance to Simpson's Farm a little further on, he heard what he thought was a slight click and felt a light tap on his back. However, he was unconcerned and arrived home without further incident. Dawson was basking in front of the fire when Kenyon returned from his outing in Clitheroe at around 11 p.m. A few words were exchanged before all went to bed for the night. The morning after, Dawson's sister Annie came into the kitchen and exclaimed, 'There's something the matter with our John, he's covered in blood.' The chair in the kitchen was also covered in blood and a trail of it led upstairs to his bedroom. John Dawson was eventually persuaded to go to hospital, where an X-ray revealed that an object about the size of a small bird's egg had penetrated his body below the shoulder blade. Dawson discharged himself from hospital, and two days later, on 22 March, he died from gangrene and other effects caused by the foreign body. To the very end, all he would say is that he did not know who had shot him. Police enquires were met with a cloak of silence from the farm workers and the villagers of Balshaw Eaves, and the strange death of John Dawson remains a mystery to this day. After this, Balshaw Eaves became known as 'the village that wouldn't talk'.

The road from the Edisford Bridge Hotel.

20 MARCH   **1857**   *Manchester Guardian* reported on a station master threatening to shoot a watchman:

> On Wednesday at the courthouse Joseph Webb, station master at Helmshore, was charged with having threatened to shoot Isaac Isherwood, watchman at Rishton Station. Some time ago, in consequence of Isherwood having given some information to the railway company respecting goods in Webb's house and which belonged to the manufacturers Harwood, Webb was removed to Helmshore. On Tuesday afternoon Webb arrived at Rishton, went to Isherwood's house and said to Isherwood 'Thou'rt a friend of mine, aren't you?' Isherwood said 'Yes' upon which Webb pulled a pistol out of his pocket and cocked it, but before he could fire it Isherwood seized him and threw him to the floor. Assistance came shortly afterwards, and the pistol was taken from him and discharged. As it was fired before being examined, it is not known whether there was a ball in it. Webb was intoxicated at the time – he was committed for trial.

21 MARCH   **1821**   The *Blackburn Mail* reported the following:

> A young man aged about 30 years of age named Robert Brown of Rimington, near Clitheroe, cut his throat with a razor. His mother left the house just a few minutes before to fetch some water, and on her return found the corpse of her unfortunate son. He had been for some time in a state of mental disarrangement.

22 MARCH   **1863**   There was a terrible accident, in which five people were killed and several seriously injured, at a new mill which was under construction in Accrington in the Woodnook area. The men were working on a scaffold inside the mill when the whole of the second and third floors gave way. Those killed were 28-year-old Brian Malone, 26-year-old James William Ingham, and 15-year-old Joseph Bradley – all of Accrington; 38-year-old William Irving of Church; and 24-year-old James Heaton of Oswaldtwistle.

23 MARCH   **1864**   A remarkable case of murder was tried at the Liverpool Assizes. One morning, in December 1863, a man named Clithero was found in bed at St Helens with Mary Wood, an unmarried woman who kept a school in town. The throats of both were cut, and the woman had been dead for some time. Clithero's wound, however, was not fatal and he was tried for the murder of his unhappy companion. The defence stated that both man and woman had mutually consented to commit suicide, and the woman had inflicted the wound herself. The prisoner was found guilty and sentenced to death.

1883 The *Lancaster Gazette* reported on a supposed murder at Slaidburn village near Clitheroe. James Purcell, a 40-year-old Irishman with a wife and five children, was charged. It appeared that Purcell was seen coming out of Mary Simpson's cottage at Slaidburn, shortly after three o'clock on 20 March 1883, then he went away with the driver of the mail cart. By late afternoon, neighbours began to worry about 65-year-old Mary, and, as the police station was across from her house, they asked PC Norton to investigate. In the upstairs bedroom he found Mary lying on the floor; she was dead, but still warm. There was blood on her right cheek, on her hand and on her right ear. A brown nebbed cap was found close by, later proved to be the cap that Purcell was wearing before he entered the cottage. Purcell was quickly traced to his abode at Eshton Terrace, Clitheroe where he was charged with manslaughter. However, at the Assizes held in April 1883, the jury returned a verdict of 'no Bill' against the prisoner.

24 MARCH

The former village police station at Slaidburn.

1865 Prior to 1800, hangings at Lancaster Castle were carried out at a place aptly called 'Gallows Hill' on the moors near the present-day Williamson Park. After this date, executions took place at the castle itself, at 'Hanging Corner'. It was here on 25 March 1865 that Stephen Burke was put to death for the murder of his wife – it was the last public hanging at the castle.

25 MARCH

1827 Rachael Bradley, a young unmarried mother, was hanged for the wilful murder of her child. Rachael left her lodging in Ashton-under-Lyne, with her illegitimate baby, to visit the overseer in the Yorkshire

26 MARCH

town where she first came from. No relief was forthcoming from the overseers at Ashton Township, and she was having difficulty feeding the child and herself. She was seen on the same day coming back from Manchester, but did not return to her lodgings until a few days later – and she was without her child. The neighbours became alarmed and accused her of having killed the child. Rachael denied this, but at length said that the wind had blown her and her child into the canal, where it had drowned. Suspicions were aroused because she had previously tried to destroy the child by giving it copperas water, but the infant had vomited it up. The police were called to drag the canal, and, on Sunday, with the consent of the canal proprietors, the navigation was drained and at last the child was found. An inquest was held at the Commercial Inn, Ashton-under-Lyne, where a verdict of 'wilful

Rachael Bradley was hanged at Lancaster Castle in March 1827.

murder' was returned and the prisoner was committed to Lancaster Castle for trial. She was executed on 26 March 1827. One cannot help thinking that Rachael was a victim of the times; she had no money and no food to feed her infant – was she going to let the poor child slowly die of starvation, or was this, in a mother's eyes, a kinder way?

1841   An inquest was held at Spotland Further Side, near Rochdale on the body of an aged man named John Ashworth. Ashworth lived next door to a woman of weak mind, named Hannah Aspinall, who was married with four or five children. Her husband, who worked away, requested that Ashworth look after his family as much as he could during his absence. Two days previous, he went into the house of the married woman and something occurred which made him strike her. She retaliated in fury, and, grabbing a piece of iron, struck Ashworth in such a manner that he died about one hour later. At the coroner's inquest, held on 27 March, a verdict of 'manslaughter' was returned, and the woman was committed to Kirkdale Prison.

27 MARCH

1872   A fearful explosion occurred at the Lovers Lane Colliery at Howe Bridge, worked by John Fletcher & Co., by which twenty-seven lives were lost. The pit, which was about 300 yards deep, worked the very fiery seam known as the Gibfield. The disaster left eleven widows and thirty-four children to mourn their loss.

28 MARCH

The Lovers Lane Colliery disaster.

FEARFUL EXPLOSION AT LOVERS LANE COLLIERY-ATHERTON. GREAT LOSS OF LIFE

1896   At the Liverpool Assizes, 70-year-old Michael White, a collier, was sentenced to four years' penal servitude for cutting the throat of his nephew, Peter White, with a razor in December 1895. It was shown that the prisoner and Peter White occupied the same bedroom, and the elder man was in the habit of rousing his victim in the mornings by sticking pins into him on various parts of the body. On the day in question, the nephew felt a strange sensation and said to the prisoner, 'You have stuck the pin rather too far this morning.' The prisoner then got a cloth, and, while pretending to wipe away the blood, seized the victim by the throat,

29 MARCH

forced his head back on the pillow, and then inflicted three large wounds across his throat. One of the wounds was serious enough for the victim to remain in hospital for a number of days.

30 MARCH 1847 An inquest was held at the Black Dog Inn, Haslingden touching on the death of 9-month-old John Chew, the son of James and Betty Chew, weavers in the town. It appeared that on the previous Saturday, the mother and father had put a large quantity of 'buff liquor', used in calico printing, and a compound of copperas and sugar of lead, on the floor. The side of the container split and the contents flowed through the cracks in the floor and onto the face and body of their child, who was asleep in the room below. The mother ran downstairs, washed the child and took him to a druggist immediately, where medicines and other curatives were administered. But the child died on Sunday evening from the effects of the poison it had swallowed. A verdict of 'accidental death' was recorded.

31 MARCH 1873 An inquest was held at the Oak Inn, Longridge on the death of a man named Henry Wilson, who was found drowned in a pit of water. He had been in low spirits for several weeks, but otherwise had not given any indication of his intent to self harm. A verdict of 'suicide whilst in an unsound state of mind' was recorded.

APRIL

The White Bull, where the inquest was held on the deaths of six mill workers killed at the Hawthorne Mill. (*See* 25 April.)

1 APRIL 1843 The *Manchester Guardian* reported:

> A circumstance occurred on Tuesday evening last, which has caused a very strong excitement in Bacup and neighbourhood. It appears that about a fortnight ago, an assault of a highly criminal nature was committed upon a girl about 11 years old, the daughter of Moses Whitehead, rope-maker of St George's Road, Bacup. A young man was accused of the offence, but immediately absconded from his residence and had not been seen since. But at dusk on Tuesday evening last, the girl was going towards home, and had reached about 50 yards of the house when she was seized by some person, who plunged a sharp instrument into her neck making three frightful wounds. As only one blow was struck, the instrument must have been of peculiar form, and the intention must have been to commit murder. Indeed the instrument narrowly missed the carotid artery, in which case certain death would have ensued. We believe that no evidence has been obtained to identify the offender, but of course under the circumstances, suspicion points strongly in a certain direction, both as to the individual who committed the crime, and the motive to suggest it.

2 APRIL 1848 An inquest was held at the Navigation Inn, Heywood touching on the death of John Diggle, a coal miner aged 43. At ten o'clock on Thursday night, he was descending in a tub at the Captain Fold Colliery when the rope broke, and the tub encountered in its fall another tub coming up – the chain attached to the latter broke his skull. He was picked up and carried to his own house, and attended to by Mr Taylor. The unfortunate man expired at one o'clock in the afternoon of the following day. The verdict was 'accidental death'.

The Navigation Inn at Heywood is now a restaurant – here, in 1848, the inquest was held on the body of John Diggle.

Elizabeth Ann Wood was killed by her husband in Oldham Road.

1867   Joseph Wood and his wife Elizabeth Ann lived at Back Ash Street, off the Oldham Road in Manchester. The marriage was not a happy one. On this day the husband, who had been out most of the day drinking, arrived home just as his wife was leaving the house. He ordered her back in and told her and the children to go to bed; a short time later he followed them up. The next morning he called a neighbour, who found Mrs Wood lying dead in a pool of blood in the bedroom. According to one of the children, Elizabeth had hidden under the bed, and when her husband found her he brutally attacked her. Wood was soon apprehended and charged with her death. In August 1867, at the Manchester Assizes, he was sentenced to twelve years for manslaughter.

3 APRIL

1893   The body of a fishmonger, found in the canal at Burnley, was named as being 50-year-old Eli Eastwood. Later, the dead body of his companion Elizabeth Longstaffe was also discovered. Both were married, but not to each other. Eastwood, having drunken habits, had fallen out with his wife over twelve months earlier, and the couple had parted. Sometime afterwards he began to cohabit with Longstaffe, and the pair took a house on Cog Lane, where they lived as man and wife. After Eastwood's body was discovered in the canal, the police broke into his house and

4 APRIL

found Elizabeth dead on the bed – her head almost severed from her body. Under the bed was a poker, bent and bloodstained, which had been used to batter her skull in. Her hand was dreadfully injured, as she had tried to

protect herself from the savage blows. Further investigation threw little light on the murder and suicide, but the couple were known to have quarrelled about money. The coroner's jury later found that Longstaffe was murdered by Eastwood, who then committed suicide.

The murdered body of Elizabeth Longstaffe, and her killer Eli Eastwood just before he committed suicide.

5 APRIL 1862 Walker Moore married his wife Betty when she was just 18, but it was not a happy marriage, and Walker was constantly argumentative and drunk. In February 1862, Betty had had enough; she left her husband and found employment at the Hare & Hounds, her uncle's public house on Skipton Old Road at Colne. Only six weeks later, Walker Moore and his companion Joseph Metcalfe calmly walked through the door of the inn. Betty gave her husband a cool reception, and although she gave him a few coppers to go to Burnley foot races the following day, she refused point blank to spend the night with him. Walker spent the night downstairs at the inn, drinking and seething in anger. The following morning, he watched as Betty went about her daily chores at

The Hare & Hounds, now renamed Black Lane Ends. It was here in April 1862 that Betty Moore had her throat slashed.

the inn. As she was on her knees cleaning the fire range, he approached her from behind, pulled back her head and sliced a razor across her throat. Poor Betty tried to stop the flow of blood with her apron, but she died within minutes. When Walker Moore was charged with the murder, he said, 'I came on purpose to do it.' Walker was found guilty of the crime and sentenced to death; the date of the execution was fixed for noon on 30 August 1862. However, Moore cheated the hangman, for on the morning of his execution he asked that he might go to use the water closet in the Chapel Yard. A few minutes later, when the wardens called out and got no reply, they found Moore had drowned himself in one of the large water cisterns. Nothing could be done to restore life, and the killer was pronounced dead by the surgeon at hand. The large crowd that had gathered outside Lancaster Castle to watch the public hanging expressed their discontent very loudly, and slowly dispersed in anger at their loss of entertainment for the day.

1944 James William Percey, a 48-year-old radio officer on the vessel **6 APRIL** *Pacific Shipper*, moored at Salford Docks, liked more than a drink or two while on shore leave. It was while he was on such a pleasure spree that he met James Galbraith in the dockland pubs of Salford. By early evening, funds were running low, and Percey suggested that they return to his ship in order to find more cash for their boozy night on the town. Galbraith followed eagerly, enticed by the mention of £60, which Percey said he had on board ship. Once on board, more drink was consumed – they even sent out an invitation to the second steward to come and join them. He promised that he would join them later, as he was at that time preoccupied. It was an hour later when the steward was able to make it to the 'party', but he found Percey's cabin locked; the man was nowhere to be seen. It was assumed that his companion in drink, James Galbraith, had simply gone ashore. The crew of the *Pacific Shipper* were well used to Percey's drinking binges, which often lasted three or four days at a time, so nobody paid much attention to the fact that he was not around. In fact, it wasn't until two days later that anyone even thought about the missing radio officer. On investigation, there were signs of blood coming from his cabin, and the door was forced open. James Percey was found with horrific head wounds caused by an axe, severe enough to cause death. Only a few coppers remained of the £60 he had on board, and they lay scattered about the deck of the cabin. Galbraith had left fingerprints all over the cabin, and was soon arrested and found guilty of the crime. On 20 July 1944, James Galbraith was hanged for murder at Manchester.

1853 The little town of Garstang was thrown into disarray when it **7 APRIL** was discovered that a murder had taken place in the quiet village. Three young men, John Wilding, William Pendlebury and Thomas Rogerson, all employed at Messrs Catterall & Co., were drinking in the Horns Inn at Garstang when a quarrel took place. The argument arose from Pendlebury telling Wilding to pay for some ale which he (Pendlebury) had ordered. The men eventually calmed down, or so it seemed, and Pendlebury and Rogerson left the inn to go home. Soon after they left, Wilding was seen running across the road with a knife in his hand. This was witnessed by a man named Benson, to whom Wilding said, 'I'm going to do for them.' Afterwards, Wilding gave Benson the knife and gave himself up to the police. A search was made in the locality and Pendlebury was found dead from a gaping wound on the inside of his thigh. A short distance away, Rogerson was found wounded on the ground. A verdict of 'wilful murder' was passed at the inquest and Wilding was sent for trial at Lancaster Assizes. In August 1853, he was found guilty of manslaughter and sentenced to transportation for twenty years.

8 APRIL 1841 At around 10.30 p.m., engine tenter Nathaniel Hibbert was returning home from work, along the Rochdale Canal at Newton Heath, when he heard a woman crying out. Running to the spot, he saw a woman in the canal. He hurried to a nearby farm and got hold of a hook, managing to get her out of the water within two minutes. But, in spite of the efforts of himself and a local druggist called Mr Race, she was declared dead. The woman was Sarah Steele, the wife of Jeremiah Steele, a shopkeeper of St George's Road. She had been parted from her husband for the last six weeks due to her addiction to alcohol. For the past three weeks she had been living in a cellar dwelling on St George's Road, and was rarely sober. On the night of her death, she went to a beer shop on Oldham Road kept by Mrs Royle – here she left a box containing a few humble possessions, saying that she would 'never see her again'. At the inquest the following Wednesday, a verdict was returned to the effect that 'the deceased drowned herself while in a state of insanity'.

9 APRIL 1856 The coroner held an inquest at the Tup Inn, on the moors between Saddleworth and Rochdale, on the body of a man found strangled in a cot on the Floxton Edge Road. From the evidence it appeared that a stonemason, Emanuel Riley, had seen a man who looked like the deceased at about half past six the previous Saturday night, a mile from the place where he was found. He appeared to be tired, walked feebly, carried his head low and had a walking stick and a bundle with him. The deceased has never been identified. He has been described as having a nose very much like the late Duke of Wellington, and small whiskers of a light sandy colour, mixed with grey hairs. He appears to have been a strongly-built man, between 60 and 70 years of age. His trousers were of woollen cord and he wore a black velveteen waistcoat, a blue swinger coat, red flannel drawers, blue cloth gaiters, a good flannel shirt, grey cotton stockings and laced shoes. The handkerchief around his neck, by which he was strangled, was a red and drab silk one. The jury returned a verdict of 'found dead'.

1822 Punishment was harsh 200 years ago, and the death penalty was administered for even the most trivial of crimes. Below are some of the sentences passed at Lancaster Crown Court on this day: 10 APRIL

> John Kay, 28, for burglary at the house of James Wilson, Oldham. DEATH
>
> James Oldham, 15, for stealing four hams at Linacre, property of R.R. Benson. DEATH
>
> George Phillips, 24; James Jones, 21; and Thomas Johnson, 23, for burglary at the house of Sarah Johnson, at Everton. DEATH
>
> Robert Hinton, 18, for horse stealing at Liverpool. DEATH
>
> William H. Sikes, 20, for uttering a bill of exchange at Liverpool with a forged endorsement therein. DEATH
>
> George Taylor, 26 and William Prescott, 24, for burglary at the house of James Webster, Ashton in Makerfield. DEATH
>
> Thomas Swodkin, 25, for stealing a mare at Liverpool. DEATH
>
> Henry Rostron, 26, for burglary at the house of E. Lord at Haslingden. DEATH
>
> James Turton, 22, for highway robbery. ACQUITTED
>
> W. Marsden, 22, for stealing three horses at Preston. DEATH
>
> Ellen Hargreaves, 30, for procuring &c. Ellen Bamfitt and Hannah Whittaker to steal a quantity of worsted stuff and cotton handkerchiefs, the property of Thomas Bamfitt and William Whittaker of Lancaster, and for receiving the said goods. SEVEN YEARS' TRANSPORTATION

1878 William Capstick was brought before Burnley County Police Court for permitting drunkenness at his house, the King's Arms at Padiham.   11 APRIL
William Stephenson and William Webster were also charged with being drunk in licensed premises. There had been a sale at the King's Arms, on 11 April, attended by around 300 people. The auctioneer noticed that several men who would be unlikely to make bids were in attendance, and he asked them to leave to make room for others. They declined, and, as an inducement, two gallons of ale were placed in another room for them to consume. When the sale was over the men rushed into the room and began to drink the spirits and glasses at will. Soon about twenty of them were stupefied, four of them so bad that they had to be conveyed home or to the police station. One man, John Stephenson, was taken home in a

cab in a state of unconsciousness, and he died the next morning having never regained consciousness. Capstick was fined £10 and the other two £1 each plus costs.

12 APRIL   **1841**   John Ashurst had been drinking for several days at Scholes, near Wigan following an argument with his wife, who left him to tend to their children. He went to bed at around 9 p.m., but a short while afterwards he got up again and went downstairs. Finding a length of stout cord, he suspended it to a ceiling beam, and, making a noose, placed it around his neck. Calling out to his young daughter that he was going to die, he kicked the chair from under his feet. His daughter hurried down to see what was happening, and was horrified to see her father hanging from the beam – she screamed; the noise alarmed the neighbours, who cut the man down. He was still alive, but he fell with such violence that his head hit a large ceramic vase, striking it with such force that it shattered. The fall and subsequent bang probably occasioned his death, which took place the following morning around noon.

13 APRIL   **1855**   Richard Pilkington, a 30-year-old weaver, and his wife Sarah, aged 29, were brought before Salford Quarter Sessions on a charge of shocking cruelty to an orphan pauper girl. Around 1851, the widowed mother of Betty Higson had died in Bolton Workhouse. A few months later, Pilkington applied to the Guardians to let him have the girl, who was then aged 9, as a servant and to learn his trade. At first he treated her well, but after about a fortnight, being dissatisfied with her work, he beat her with a stick, wounding her back and causing blood to flow. Pilkington's wife was witness to this but took no action. Since that time he beat the girl almost constantly, and did not give her enough food. Although she was a strong girl when she left the workhouse, she was later found to be weak and emaciated – perhaps, according to the prosecution, even beyond recovery. On one occasion, he seized her by the neck and then held her within inches of the fire for some time. On at least two occasions he denied her when she asked to attend the calls of nature, probably brought about by the brutal treatment she received, and afterwards he forced her to lick the filth from the floor. The chairman sentenced Richard Pilkington to six months' imprisonment and his wife was discharged. The case caused a great deal of excitement in the neighbourhood of Bolton.

14 APRIL   **1840**   Poor 20-year-old Julia Wareing, of Bolton, had not had a good life. At an early age she had a severe attack of measles, and since then appeared mentally disturbed. She lost the use of an eye, and was often in low spirits. A chance to uplift the poor creature came in 1838, when

she got married, but it was not to be – her husband left her after three weeks. To make matters worse, her parents, vexed at the marriage breaking up, refused to acknowledge her and she was forced to obtain work as a domestic servant. Suffering from further depression, the unfortunate lass took some laudanum – but on this occasion medical assistance intervened. She continued to be in low spirits from that time onwards. At around one o'clock on 14 April 1840, she got a young girl to accompany her to Mr Watson, a surgeon of Deansgate. Here she bought two ounces of arsenic, on the pretence that she had been plagued by rats and needed the poison to kill them off. When she arrived home she went into the cellar of the house, locking the door behind her, and swallowed the poison. Suspicions were aroused by some neighbours, who, on breaking down the cellar door, found Julia Wareing seated on a chair – she confessed to having taken the arsenic, and once again surgical aid was procured. However, this time it was too late – Julia died at about seven o'clock in the evening. A verdict was returned at the inquest of 'temporary insanity'.

1843   Simeon Cropper, a young man in the employ of Robert Lees at the   15 APRIL
Hogshead Colliery at Bacup, was sent out with two horses and two carts to the saddler shop belonging to Timothy Nelson. The carts needed some repairs, as did the harness for one of the horses. The halter and collar were duly taken off the horse, and, being of liberty and still attached to the cart, the horse suddenly turned around and galloped along the footpath on the other side of the street. Having gained some speed, the horse passed close to the shop windows of grocer George Stewart, where, at that very same moment, 8-year-old Henry Monk and his brother, a child of just 3, were passing over the threshold of the premises. Both were instantly knocked to the ground, and the wheels of the cart passed over both young bodies. The impact broke the back of Henry Monk, and he died within three hours of his injuries. The younger boy had his arms crushed, and other wounds about his body. An inquest held at the Waterloo Hotel later returned a verdict of 'accidental death' on the child.

1833   William Durham, aged 32, pleaded guilty to a charge of stealing   16 APRIL
a sack and a tin can at Burnley, and two pairs of shoes and two silk handkerchiefs at Cliviger. He had twice been convicted at previous hearings and had even broken out of jail before. The chairman at the Session said that Durham had had enough warnings. He felt that the court would not be doing its duty if they permitted him to remain in this country, and therefore sentenced him to be transported for the term of fourteen years.

17 APRIL, 1851   There was considerable excitement in and around Clitheroe as a rabid dog was running around and snapping at everything that came its way. The dog was a cur and came from the direction of Grindleton. On entering Clitheroe, it was met by a man named Smalley, whom it bit severely on the leg. The strange dog then came along Church Brow and down Church Street, where it ran into Mr Barton's doorway. It was chased up Castle Street, along Salford and Long Row, and towards Henthorne. A number of dogs were bitten along the way and nearly all of them had to be destroyed.

18 APRIL, 1853   Richard Pedder, a boatman on the Preston to Lancaster Canal, entered the Shovels Inn at Hambleton and announced to the assembled crowd within, 'I have just killed our Bet.' A number of the men in the pub then went to Pedder's house to see if this was true. They were met with the lifeless body of Betty Pedder lying in the garden – she had been shot and was lying in a pool of blood. Soon afterwards Pedder returned, shaking and weeping. He tried to take his own life with the shotgun, but this was quickly removed from him by the men present. Soon the police were on the spot and they arrested Pedder and charged him with the murder. Pedder was wild and excitable, and all he could do was keep

The Shovels Inn, where Richard Pedder announced that he had killed his wife.

repeating, 'I am a good shot; I aimed for the killing place, and that was her head.' The jury at the trial returned a verdict of 'wilful murder' and the death sentence was duly passed upon him by Mr Justice Wightman. It was suggested that Pedder had committed the crime on impulse, or while the balance of his mind was upset. A petition was raised to try and reprieve the condemned man, but the Home Secretary was unmoved. On 27 August 1853, William Calcraft, the hangman, slipped the noose over Pedder's head, and a moment later it was all over.

1844 The *Preston Guardian* reported on the poor treatment of some **19 APRIL** orphan children. A widow of Middleton had died and left eight children; Jonathan and James were placed in the Middleton Workhouse. In March, the boys were put into the care of a coal miner at Walmsley-cum-Shuttleworth near Bury, who agreed to take them as parish apprentices on a six-week trial and pay them 2s 6d per week. A few weeks later the boys' relations went to see them, after hearing how the boys had been treated of late. The elder lad had two black eyes and his ears were torn in a most brutal manner; nearly the whole of his body was covered in wounds. The younger lad was not quite so ill-used, but both had been beaten by their master in the coal pit because they could not perform the work to his satisfaction. The boys were taken back to Middleton in a most filthy condition.

1833 A number of soldiers of the 85th Foot Regiment, stationed at the **20 APRIL** barracks in Salford, were ordered to escort a deserter from the New Bailey (Manchester) to Liverpool, under the command of Corporal Naggs. As the soldiers approached Warrington, the men were invited in for breakfast at the home of the deserter, and they took up the offer. One of the soldiers, a Private Roach, asked Corporal Naggs if he might take off the handcuffs restraining the prisoner. Corporal Naggs replied in the negative – at which Roach got rather angry, and turned to his fellow soldiers, saying they were 'no men, for suffering a prisoner to get his breakfast with handcuffs on, while they had loaded muskets'. The Corporal warned Roach to be careful, and said that if he interfered with the prisoner, or encouraged others to do the same, he would be on a charge. The matter appears to have been dropped and the men continued on their journey, arriving back at the barracks in Salford around 9 p.m. the following Monday. Within the hour Private Roach was arrested, his musket was unloaded and he was placed in the guardhouse. The following morning he was allowed out on parade – this lasted about half an hour, but when the parade was over, instead of going back to the guardhouse he went to the barracks room where Corporal Naggs was in conversation with another Private. Roach looked him straight in the eye and said, 'I'm obliged to you Corporal Naggs for what you have done to me.' The Corporal replied, 'John, it is your own fault.' With that, Roach pulled out a musket and fired it point blank into the chest of Corporal Naggs. The officer staggered back a few yards and then fell back, fatally injured. Roach was arrested soon after by some other soldiers who had heard the musket going off – he never denied his actions. He repeated over and over, 'It was I who done it, I shot the Corporal!' At the inquest, a verdict of 'wilful murder' was returned against Roach, who was sent for trial at Lancaster Castle. He was found guilty, and executed at Lancaster on 17 August 1833.

21 APRIL **1855**   At West Leigh, 16-year-old Margaret Gregson, an embroiderer at a factory, suffered a fatal accident. Returning to work after dinner, she and four other girls had to cross the Bolton & Kenyon Junction Railway. A train was approaching at the time, and two of the girls shouted to Gregson not to follow as the train was so near. Not hearing, or simply not heeding, she attempted to cross the line. As she was taking the last step off it, she was struck by the buffer of the engine and thrown forward a considerable distance. Her ribs were broken, and she survived the accident only half an hour. An inquest held on Monday recorded a verdict of 'accidental death'.

22 APRIL **1815**   George Lyon, the Upholland Highwayman, was 54 when he was executed along with William Houghton and David Bennett. Another accomplice, Edward Ford, had suggested to Lyon that they rob Walmsley House, where Ford worked; this was the robbery for which Lyon and his accomplices were eventually indicted. Ford had taken part in some seventeen previous robberies, but because he turned King's Evidence, he was spared the capital sentence. The execution of Lyon, Houghton, and Bennett took place just before noon on Saturday, 22 April 1815. The hanging was recorded in the *Lancaster Gazette* on 29 April 1815 as follows:

> On Saturday last about noon, George Lyon, David Bennett and William Houghton convicted at our last assizes of burglary near Wigan underwent the awful sentence of the law on the drop behind our castle. Houghton was first brought on the platform and seemed to pray most fervently, as did the others, especially Lyon, who was the last tied up, and was dressed in black with topped boots. After hanging the usual time the bodies were taken down and given to their friends for interment.

23 APRIL **1850**   William Sixsmith was committed to trial on a number of offences, including night poaching, being armed, and shooting – with intent to kill

– at Richard Redhead, gamekeeper at Knowsley. It appeared that there were four gamekeepers at Knowsley, and they observed four poachers whom they tried to apprehend. After a serious affray three of them got away, Sixsmith being the only one secured. Redhead was shot at whilst he was down, his face being only about a yard from the mouth of the gun at the time it went off; the rim of his hat was blown off. Sixsmith was also charged with stabbing a constable about ten years ago.

1555 Smithills Hall, one of Bolton's museums, became the home of the wealthy, sheep-owning Barton family in 1485, and remained so for almost 200 years. In 1554, local farmer George Marsh was brought before Robert Barton, the owner of the estate, after he was tried for being a Protestant during the reign of devoted Catholic, Mary Tudor. Tradition says that, as George Marsh was leaving the hall, he stamped his foot on the floor and left a footprint on the stone flags which has remained there ever since. On 24 April 1555, he was burned at the stake for his beliefs. The Green Room where Marsh was questioned is reputed to be the most haunted room at Smithills Hall, and the footprint is said to run with blood on the anniversary of his death.

24 APRIL

Smithills Hall.

1855 Hawthorne Mill stood beside Folly Brook, on the very edge of the moors and to the East of the main road running between Rawtenstall and Burnley. The cotton mill was four storeys high, with a boiler house. At the far end, separated by a stout wall, was a room used as the smithy and mechanics' shop at the mill. Above this room was a space occupied by a number of winding frames. In 1855, the mill was being worked by Messrs Giles and George Pilkington. On Wednesday 25 April, the steam engine was stopped at dinnertime – as was usual – and restarted at 1.30 after all the hands had returned from dinner. At 3.20 there was a terrific explosion as the mill boiler blew up. The engineer, Roger Holden, was sitting within a few yards of the firing end of the boiler house; he was very severely scalded, but, because of his position, he escaped being hit by any of the debris. In fact, he was able to walk home after the incident and was fully expected to recover. Eight females who were working in the room containing the winding frames also escaped injury, but six people in the mechanics' shop and the smithy were killed in the blast. Those killed were Samuel Fort, a scavenger aged 57; Edward Mitchell, a blacksmith aged 34; Richard Burton, a 22-year-old unmarried mechanic; Abraham Nowell, an overlooker aged 26; William Barnes,

25 APRIL

a 16-year-old smith's apprentice; and poor Robert Holden, a smith's apprentice aged just 13 years.

An inquest into the accident, which became known as the 'Crawshawbooth Tragedy', was held at the White Bull public house on the main road at Crawshawbooth on 4 May 1855. Mr George Pilkington, one of the partners in the firm, was in attendance, but the jury objected to his presence and the coroner asked that he remove himself. It appeared that, a short time before the explosion, in order to increase the power to the steam engines the pressure at the boiler was increased from 28lb per square inch to 36lb per square inch. However, these changes were made by respectable engineers sent by Mr Walker of Bury. There was a great deal of debating as to what might have been the cause of the explosion, and after adjournments and a great deal of deliberation over whether or not to include the word 'accidental', the jury eventually recorded the following verdict: 'The deaths were caused by the bursting of a steam boiler, but from what cause we cannot ascertain.' By all accounts the mill did survive, although it was marked as 'disused' on a 1930s' map. In later years Hawthorn Mill was owned by Hollingsworth Bros Ltd, a part of the Pressed Felt group, and was used for jute processing. It was badly damaged by a fire on Saturday, 21 July 1962 and most of the building was declared unsafe. The mill was then demolished in early September 1962, and the chimney was felled on 17 September by Thomas McHugh of Bury. There are no remains of Hawthorne Mill left; the area is now a grassy field with nothing to show of the terrible day when six men and boys perished in an explosion at the mill.

26 APRIL **1817** The 'Pendleton Murders' caused an enormous amount of excitement in the Manchester district at the time they were committed. The two victims were Margaret Marsden, aged 75, and Hannah Partington, aged 20 – two servant girls in the well-to-do household of a merchant named Thomas Littlewood. They were found viciously murdered at the house of their employer on 26 April 1817. The motive for the crime appeared to have been robbery; silverware and clothing, as well as a great deal of money, had been taken from the property. The alleged culprits were soon brought to justice. They were James Ashcroft; his son, also named James; their brother and uncle respectively, David Ashcroft; and William Holden. They were found guilty of the offence, and the usual sentence was passed upon them. All four men denied the murders from the moment they were arrested, in the courts and even on the scaffold. Their refusal to admit guilt was looked upon with horror; the opinion was that those about to go to God should at least have the grace to admit their guilt and beg forgiveness. This led many people at the hangings to believe that they were indeed innocent of the crime.

1855 There was great alarm at Clitheroe when the body of a young child was found in Wilkin Brook, Low Moor in the town. The inquest heard how Jonathan Bowker was playing with another lad in John Hargreave's Meadow near Wilkin Brook. Bowker went to the side of the brook close to the bridge, over the road leading to Mercer's Mill, and in the water he saw a child. It was lying face-down and its back was out of the water. He and James Nowell pulled the body out with a stick; they did not know what it was at the time. The body was quite naked, and they stayed with it until the police arrived. The face was blackish and seemed very much swollen. Evidence from the surgeon informed the inquest that the child was a full-grown infant, but was in such a state of decomposition that it was impossible to define the cause of death. Other witnesses gave evidence, but at the end the jury returned a verdict that: 'The deceased male child was found in Wilkin Brook, but by what means it came to its death there was no evidence to show.'

27 APRIL

1853 An inquest was held at the Bay Horse Inn, Baxenden touching on the death of Edmund Pilling, who had died on the previous Tuesday from supposed injuries inflicted by William Grimshaw, a labourer. On that day, a man calling himself Richard had left a ferret with the landlady, with instructions that she should keep hold of it until he returned. 'Richard' had barely left the house when Grimshaw demanded the ferret, but the landlady refused to give it up. He then attempted to take it by force, but

28 APRIL

The Bay Horse Inn.

the landlady stood her ground and called out to some of the regular customers for assistance. The first to answer the call was Edmund Pilling. A scuffle followed, during which time the landlady fetched her husband. For a time all was quiet, and the men returned to the kitchen area of the hotel, Pilling sitting down upon a bench. A few seconds later, Grimshaw ran across the room and, with a 'kicking punch', struck Pilling with a violent blow to the left leg. The limb was broken and the man had to be conveyed home on a cart. He was attended to by Dr Crosby, but died a few days later. The doctor stated at the inquest that the cause of death was pleural pneumonia and that the broken limb had nothing to do with his demise. The coroner, though, summed up the case and returned a verdict of 'manslaughter' against Grimshaw. At the Lancaster Summer Assizes held in August, it was found that William Grimshaw had no bill to answer and his case was dismissed.

29 APRIL 1847 James Needham, a farmer and beer seller of Block Lane near Oldham, was summoned before the petty sessions to show why his aged father was chargeable to the township of Chadderton. The overseer stated that the sum due from the defendant was 1s per week. The defendant stated that he was unable to pay the sum, for he only had 12s per week to keep himself, and he had a wife and several children to keep. His eldest son was a power loom weaver with two looms at Werneth Mill, but he was only working two and a half days a week. Needham admitted under questions from the Bench that he farmed nine acres of land, and paid £30 a year in rent. The defendant was told that he must settle the case in a fortnight otherwise proceedings would be taken against him. Thomas Needham, brother of the defendant, was then charged with refusing to contribute in a like manner to support his aging father. The overseer said that four months' pay was due from him. The defendant said that he was a silk weaver and had a wife and four children; silk weaving was going through a very bad time, and it would be three or four weeks before he would receive any money. His family was not bringing in half of what they were two months since, and he had not a shilling to himself since last Easter. The case was adjourned for a fortnight, and the defendant was ordered to see what he could do in the meantime.

30 APRIL 1846 William Leeson, aged 20, was employed as an engine tenter at his father's lime works near Belle Vue, Gorton. He had been at work all day on a twelve-hour shift and was about to go home. However, when he left the engine house there were three men at work, one repairing the teeth of a cog wheel, and two others repairing the arm of the drum. None of the men saw William Leeson leave, but soon noticed unusual noises coming from the enginehouse; the engine was running erratically. The men rushed outside to see what was amiss, and saw the body of William Leeson between the wheels which connected with the shafting outside the building. Witnesses at the inquest later said: 'The body of the deceased fell out on the other side of the wheels, literally crushed flat, the head being a perfect mummy and presented a most horrible sight.' The jury at the inquest, after a short deliberation, returned a verdict of 'accidental death'.

MAY

Waddington village was the scene of a murder in 1833. (*See* 16 May.)

1 MAY   **1833**   The Duke of Manchester coach was on its way between Manchester and Preston when one of the axels broke whilst descending a hill about 2 miles from Bolton. One of the passengers was injured a great deal, and two or three others were hurt to a lesser extent. The *Manchester Guardian* concluded:

> No blame was attributable to the driver, but we cannot suffer the occasion to pass without strongly impressing upon coach proprietors the necessity of paying the strictest attention to so an important part of a coach as the wheel axles. They ought to be made of the very best iron, and submitted to severe trial of their strength and soundness before being used. We have heard of no fewer than six accidents within as many months, owing entirely to defects in the materials or workmanship of the axle-trees on stage coaches.

2 MAY   **1840**   Thomas Haslam, alias 'Bullock', was brought before the Bench charged with stealing a horse belonging to Henry Scholes, butcher of Great Bolton. Scholes stated that on 11 September 1839, he was at Ormskirk Fair with a horse for sale, when the prisoner came up to him and said, 'You do not show that horse off [at its best] to my mind, I can make better of it.' Scholes then gave the horse to the prisoner for the exhibition, and told him that if he got a customer, Haslam should bring him to the Lower Gates Inn, where he (Scholes) would be waiting for him. Scholes waited for some time, but Haslam did not appear, and at length he came to the conclusion that he had sold the beast and spent his winnings. When questioned, Scholes thought that the horse was probably worth around £10, but had been informed that Haslam had sold it for £2. Haslam was committed for trial at the Salford Sessions.

3 MAY   **1887**   At Burnley Police Court, a weaver named James Fielding was brought before the magistrates on a charge of having deserted his wife and three children on 15 August 1885. John Hargreaves, the relieving officer, gave evidence of the prisoner's desertion and the fact that his family had been relieved to the sum of £4. In answer to the Bench, the prisoner stated that he had left his wife and sold her to another man for 1½ *d*. The man to whom he had sold her was living with her and had children by her. It was owing to his wife's misbehaviour with other men that he had left her. He was committed to prison for fourteen days, with liberty to settle with the relieving officer.

4 MAY   **1868**   An old man named Richard Croston, of High Street, Preston, was cleaning an old gun he owned and had placed it in front of the fire to soften the oil before sitting down to breakfast. He had not been sat down for many minutes when the gun, which unbeknown to him was loaded, exploded. A piece of the barrel struck Croston in the jugular vein, killing him instantly. His wife, who was on the other side of the table, escaped without any injuries.

1834 Richard Fowler of Ashton was aware of an unwelcome colony of rats amongst the wheat in his barn, and he assembled a number of men and dogs to hunt them out. Some nests of young ones were first discovered and these were destroyed. On removing the last of the wheat bales, ninety-seven large rats presented themselves, and, being unable to escape, gave battle with the dogs. The contest lasted an hour and a half, eighty-eight of the enemy being killed on the spot and seven taken prisoner; two escaped alive. The suspicion of the farmer that his golden crop was infested with rats was thus ratified! *5 MAY*

1838 The sexton was digging a grave in St Mary's churchyard in Lancaster when, at a depth of about 6ft, he discovered a copper coin about the size of the halfpenny of the day, only much thicker. Antiquarians who have seen it suggest it might be of the coins of Empress Faustina, wife of Antoninus Pius. She died in 141, aged 37, so the coin must have been at least 1,697 years old! *6 MAY*

1855 At the borough court at Bolton, two rough-looking men from Little Lever – a collier named William Simons, and a boat builder named Thomas Waters – were charged with an assault upon William Cross, and subsequently upon the police at the Ship Inn taproom. The incident occurred at about eleven o'clock the previous Saturday night. The case was rendered remarkable by the palpable perjury of two of the witnesses – it was proved by the complainant William Cross, who was hardly able to walk from injuries received from the accused, and by Mr and Mrs Calderbank (the keepers of the taproom), that these men went to the house drunk and created a disturbance. Calderbank ordered them out and they became so violent that he had to fetch the police. They then both set upon Cross and knocked him down. When Calderbank returned with one of the policemen, they were both still on top of Cross, and when the officer dragged them off they knocked him down and kicked him also. Higson, another officer who arrived at the scene, had his thumb bitten by Waters. The defence then called upon a youth named Robert Grundy, and Alice Simon, sister of one of the accused, who swore that the defendants never struck Cross at all, and that they only 'chucked him off the bench'. Grundy admitted that they got the policeman down, but the girl stoutly maintained that the policeman fell by himself and was not struck or kicked by her brother. *7 MAY*

Both accused were fined £5 for each assault upon the policemen or, in default, two months' imprisonment.

8 MAY **1848** Reports indicated that an old water mill at Barton-on-Irwell had been destroyed by fire. Barton Old Mill, a quaint-looking and somewhat picturesque edifice, stood in a hollow near Barton Bridge and was occupied by John Jones & Co., corn millers. At one point during the fire, fears were expressed for three of Mr Jones's children who were sleeping in an adjoining cottage, and there was great difficulty rescuing them from the inferno. The origin of the fire was attributed to friction on one of the shafts.

9 MAY **1891** An inquest was held at the police courts in Blackpool on Mary Ann Farnsworth of Feniscowles, Blackburn, who was killed at Blackpool Central Station the previous Monday. Monica Graham, her sister, said that on the day in question, there was a vast crowd on the platform. As the train backed into the station, several people got hold of the handles and ran along with the train – during this rush, her sister slipped down between two of the carriages. Monica said, 'On that day the crowds were almost wild, and they climbed over the barriers.' The jury returned a verdict of 'accidental death'.

10 MAY **1854** An inquest was held on the body of James Ainscough, who for several years had held the post of assistant overseer of Wigan. It appeared that the deceased had been drinking for some time and, as a result, was seized with *delirium tremens*. At about seven o'clock on the Saturday prior to his death, he got out of bed and inflicted a frightful gash on the right side of his throat. The surgeon was called, who treated the gash by stitching the wound and applying bandages, but Mr Ainscough only survived until about one o'clock the following day.

11 MAY **1834** Richard Brown, who was residing with his farmer father in the Pendle Forest, was killed by a cow which he was leading into another field. It was supposed that the animal turned restive and kicked the man in the breast – he died almost immediately.

12 MAY **1840** A young man named Nicholas Fox and a woman named Sarah Bell were brought before the court and charged with robbery. John Walsh of Blakeley Street, Manchester stated that, being a stranger in town, he had lost his way and ended up in a whiskey vault which was full of women; he paid for some liquor for some of them, although he only stayed a few minutes. On removing himself from the premises he was followed out by Bell, who got hold of his collar. He tried to push her

away but another man came up and knocked him to the ground. Whilst he was down the man stole his purse, which contained a sovereign and a sixpence piece. He called out, and a man came to his assistance. Francis Flinn stated that, at about 12.30 in the afternoon, he heard a cry of 'murder' in St George's Road. He then saw Walsh on the ground with Fox and Bell upon him. He secured both of the prisoners and handed them over to a police officer. Both prisoners denied that they had tried to rob Walsh, but nevertheless they were committed for trial.

1840 An aged female named Betty Brooks, who resided at 'Hag End' 13 MAY at Haulgh, was interred at the Parish Church, Bolton – and by her own directions in a very singular manner. Her husband died in 1825, and from that time up until her death she took great care of his clothes. His two coats were brushed every day, and his shoes and clogs were polished regularly. The pillow on which his head had rested at the time of his death was a particularly special item to Betty. By her orders, the shoes were placed at her feet in the coffin, the coats were laid under her body, and the pillow under her head; a clog was placed under each arm. In this manner she was interred.

1847 A respectable-looking woman by the name of Eliza Ann 14 MAY Burroughs was brought before the borough court at Bolton charged with stealing a set of coral beads from the neck of a little girl, the daughter of John Dutton of Deansgate. The child stated that on the previous Tuesday, the woman had approached her and asked if her mother wanted a servant. She then took her down Ridgeway Gates and plaited her hair, and when the girl got home the beads were missing. The next day, the child pointed out the young woman, who had the beads around her neck. In a statement, she claimed to have found the beads in Ridgeway Gates, and did not know that the child had lost them. Having previously been of good character, the woman was then dismissed.

1886 Alfred Bligh, a 31-year-old ex-police constable from Kirkham, 15 MAY murdered his own children. Bligh's wife had died in December 1884, and his wife's sister, Annie Turner, had agreed to look after the house and the children for him. However, she left the following September, and in November gave birth to an illegitimate child of which Alfred Bligh was the father. He paid her a certain sum of money towards the keep of the child, but she took out a summons for affiliation – this led to him having to resign from the police force. From then on, Bligh became more and more depressed. He wrote a letter to his wife's sister before the murders, in which he stated:

You have brought me into a nice mess. You have been advised by other people so you can go to them to keep you and the child. You have got me dismissed from the police force, so you will have to keep the child yourself. When you get this letter I shall be cold. It is all through you summonsing me. I told you long ago if you ever did do it I would not pay you anything, so I have made away with all of us.

On 15 May 1886, while the housekeeper was out of the house, Bligh strangled his three little daughters, 6-year-old Lily, 4-year-old Gertrude and 18-month-old Nellie – he then fractured their skulls with an axe. The funerals of the poor little innocents took place a few days later, in the parish church at Kirkham. The sad spectacle was watched by thousands, and included many friends of the little girls. Finally, Bligh cut his own throat with a razor and then jumped out of the bedroom window. Remarkably he survived, and was taken to court where his defence was insanity. The jury found him guilty of murder and sentenced him to death. However, in July 1886 it was reported that his death sentence had been reprieved.

16 MAY 1833   Waddington is a pretty Ribble Valley village not far from Clitheroe in East Lancashire – a lovely rural scene today, but one of murder on 16 May 1833. On this day, Mary Whitehead saw William Southworth go into the butcher's shop belonging to 53-year-old Robert Chatburn. The latter was beating his wife – she was crying out and Southworth asked Chatburn to stop. Taking hold of Chatburn, he pushed him towards a chair. Both men fell over the chair and landed on the ground; whilst still on the floor, the village constable, John Pinder, arrived and asked what was going on. Southworth said to Chatburn, 'Now Robert, if thou will be quiet, thou shall get up – I have no ill feeling against thee.' They both got up off the floor, although there was still an uneasy tension in the air. Chatburn then said that he had a calf to kill, and Southworth said that he would help him kill the calf. The men left together. Robert Chatburn killed the calf, and then threw his whittle (knife) across the room. He was still in a vicious mood, and, collecting some hot water, he threw this into a crowd of women and children who had gathered in the street. He then threw the basin to his wife, who managed to catch it. Chatburn's wife said that William Southworth would not have helped Chatburn kill the calf if he knew what her husband had been saying. Southworth replied that if he heard Chatburn say such things again he would 'lick him'. Chatburn promptly marched back to the slaughterhouse, returned with his whittle, and said to Southworth, 'What sayest thou?' Southworth replied, 'If thou sayest that I have been too kind with thy wife, I'll lick thee.' Chatburn then rushed at Southworth; a struggle ensued and Southworth fell to the ground with a stab wound in his back. Not content with that, Chatburn carried on beating the man until the knife was taken off him by some of the men folk. Southworth was taken home but died there soon after. Robert Chatburn was tried at York Assizes on 19 July 1833, found guilty of manslaughter and sentenced to be transported for life.

1885 In Bolton-by-Bowland, 26-year-old Grace Isherwood and her sister Isabella Gardiner, a domestic servant in Dalton, were charged with the wilful murder of 2-year-old Thomas Gardiner. Isherwood was married to a farmer in Meanley, near Slaidburn, but she had concealed the fact that she had an illegitimate son whom she was having nursed at Dalton in Furness. Her sister brought the child back to her, and it became necessary for Isherwood to explain to her husband to whom the boy belonged. She hastily explained that her sister Isabella was looking after the boy for another person. On 17 May, an attempt was made to get the child into Clitheroe Workhouse, but this proved unsuccessful. The pair then supposedly drowned the infant in Easington Beck, about 2 miles from where Isherwood lived. At the Assizes on 4 August 1885, however, the jury found the sisters 'not guilty' of the offence and they were discharged. 17 MAY

1864 An inquest was held at the Victoria Hotel, Glasson Dock, Thurnham upon the body of 63-year-old W. Escolme, who was found in the canal basin the previous day. The deceased was a native of Cockermouth, but had been an inmate at Lancaster Union Workhouse for many years, and had only left at the end of the previous week. Since then he had been drinking whenever he could get hold of alcohol. It being Whitsuntide, he had met many old friends, who had given him a glass for 'Auld Lang Syne'. For the last two or three days of his life he had been drinking at the Victoria Hotel, and at nights he slept in some outhouses belonging to the establishment. His coat, cap and stick were found on the bank of the basin, close to where the body was found, which gave rise to the thinking that he might have committed suicide. There was, however, no evidence to show that this was the case and a verdict of 'found drowned' was returned. 18 MAY

1847 The *Manchester Guardian* reported on the detection of some coiners at Bolton. On the previous Monday, at about 9.30 p.m., a man named George Peter Bowen went to the shop of Mr Higson, an ironmonger in Deansgate, and bought a white metal table spoon. The appearance and conduct of the man excited Mr Higson and he sent his son after him; the man was traced to 7 King Street. Information was given to the police 19 MAY and Superintendent Harris and Sergeants Beech and Mewburn visited the suspect's house. They found George Peter Bowen, his wife Catherine Bowen, his daughter Mary Bowen, lodger Mary Mitchell, and three children – two belonging to the Bowens and the other to Mitchell. In Catherine Bowen's left hand they found three bad shillings, and, on the table, the new spoon which Bowen had bought from Mr Higson. Sergeant Mewburn found some white metal, powdered plaster of Paris, and other coining material around the house. Mr Harris also found a base shilling on the floor, and Mary Mitchell was seen throwing something into the fire. When the fire was put out, four bad shillings were found among the ashes. The suspects were all taken before the mayor, and Edmund Ashworth Esq., and the above facts were detailed as evidence, whereby the prisoners were committed for trial at the next Assizes. The prisoners pleaded not to be separated from their children, and at length the magistrates included the three children in the committal, so that they might all go to prison together.

20 MAY 1871 Two colliers, William Henderson and John Scott, entered the house of Peter Brown of Pemberton. Henderson struck the table with a thick stick, saying to Brown, 'Money or murder you.' He then dealt Brown a vicious blow on the head, and laid the stick on the table. Scott picked up the stick and Henderson seized a poker; with that, Henderson started beating Brown in a most violent way – the pair kicked him and also tried to strangle him. Henderson then tried to gouge out Brown's eyes with his thumbs – and perhaps would have succeeded if not for the intervention of a butcher named Fairhurst. The injured man was attended to by Mr Sandell, and for some time was in a dangerous state. His attackers were committed for trial at the Quarter Sessions.

21 MAY 1844 Following information received from members of the public, Richard Goodhind, an agent for the Excise, went to the residence of Thomas Waddacre at his farm called Haydock's, near Over Darwen, with a search warrant. Goodhind found a boiler in the back kitchen and, in a field to the rear of the farm, found bottles of illicit spirits, various 'worms' and a still head. Following a later and more detailed search by Constable Samuel Butterworth, they discovered fifteen holes in the field containing bottles, parts of the still and wash. In his defence of Waddacre, Robert Grime said that Waddacre was a member of a Sick Club, and that since Christmas Waddacre had been five or six months on the sick, and had generally been confined to bed. The magistrates, however, were not convinced, and charged Waddacre the full penalty of £200.

1868 Reports were made of a shocking murder committed on 20 May 1868 at Salford. The scene of the crime was 38 Wood Street, the home of the Donaghue family and their three children. Late at night, screams of murder were heard coming from the house – but because these had been heard before, none of the neighbours took any notice. Around seven o'clock the following morning, the husband was seen coming out of the house covered in blood; in his hand was a clasp knife. As a crowd gathered to see what was going on, he raised his hands and shouted, 'There's one gone, and soon there will be another.' Mrs Donaghue was found inside the house, dead, and her husband was arrested. At the station the man appeared to faint, and when examined was found to have deep wounds to his left side, inflicted by himself. For a time he was in a dangerous condition, but he did rally enough to face the charge of manslaughter in August 1868 – he was found guilty and sentenced to ten years' penal servitude.

22 MAY

A frantic scene of murder being committed in the Donaghue household.

1853 A quantity of bone – an almost perfect skeleton of a child 4 or 5 years of age – was discovered on Gallows Hill, Lancaster. Some years ago, not far from this spot, the headless bodies of some of the rebels of the 1745 Rebellion were discovered.

23 MAY

1868 William and Harriet Thompson, man and wife, were brought before the Blackburn Police Court charged with ill-treating Harriet's son, William Henry Duxbury. The child in question was found in a back room, securely fastened in a chest 14½in deep, 25in long and 18in wide. The lid was closed and the child had been in that cramped position without food since half past five in the morning. Each of the prisoners had three children with previous partners before they married each other; the eldest was not more than nine years old. Statements from the other children indicated that they often went without food for whole days. The parents were sentenced to six months' imprisonment and the children were placed in a workhouse.

24 MAY

25 MAY   **1868**   An inquest was held at the Black Bull Inn, Kirkham, on the body of traveller Charles Brown, aged about 45, who committed suicide by cutting his throat. The deceased lived at Eccles and had come to see his father at Kirkham on the previous Wednesday. He complained of being tired and afterwards poorly. Later on, his sister took him a cup of tea, noticed blood on the blankets and ran downstairs. It was discovered that he had cut his throat with a knife, and he lived for about three quarters of an hour after his sister had found him. There were cuts upon his cheeks and on his arms also. The jury returned a verdict that he had committed suicide while in an unsound state of mind.

26 MAY   **1861**   Poor Mary Grimes, a young girl who lived in the vicinity of Leyland, was found drowned in a pit of water. It appeared that the girl lived with Mr J. Bateson, a yeoman, and worked as a farm servant. She had found herself pregnant, and, rather than be a burden on anyone, or perhaps to keep the child's paternity secret, she chose to end her young life. Attached to her bonnet, beside the water where she had drowned, was the following pitiful letter:

> Dear father and mother, pardon me for this rash act I am now about to commit. If I should live any longer in this world I shall become troublesome to someone, and that is not my wish by a great deal. All I crave is that you shall forgive me for what I have done amiss to you and see that I am buried somewhere which ever you think most proper. If you will fetch my box away from Mr Bateson's you will find three pound in the small purse. You must take that towards my expenses, which I hope will not be so very heavy, and you will give the box and all these clothes to my two sisters, and I wish them health to wear them. I do not know that I crave of anything in this world now, as I have but a few friends, but it was once not the case. If only I had one spare hour I could talk much better than to write, but it is too late now, for my time is short. In a few hours I will pass into eternity, and shall do no more as one which is at present very unhappy, but quite sensible at present.
> Yours
> Mary Grimes
> Clayton-le-Woods, aged twenty three years.

27 MAY   **1883**   Ruth Mary Hodgson was walking down Watling Street, Fulwood, and noticed a young couple coming towards her. There appeared to be no conversation between the young lovers, but the girl walked away from the man twice before passing Ruth. A few minutes later, Ruth heard a loud report, and looking up Albert Road saw the young woman fall to the ground. The young man looked at the fallen girl and then

stood up straight. Ruth heard another shot – the man staggered slightly backwards and fell into the hedge. A crowd quickly gathered, alerted by the gunshots and the commotion, and the brigade surgeon at Fulwood Barracks soon arrived. Some onlookers held the girl up, and a pistol shot wound was found behind the girl's right ear, from which blood and brain matter were oozing – the young man was already dead. The girl remained unconscious until her death at 1.30 a.m. the following day. The young girl was named as Mary Yates, aged 20 years, a servant in the employ of Mr James Wilding, a manufacturer on Watling Street. The young man was James Brocklehurst Proctor, aged 22 years, a solicitor's clerk employed by John Catterall at Winckley Street Preston. An inquest into the deaths was held on 29 May 1883, at Fulwood Workhouse – but there was no real evidence to explain why James shot his young lover, to whom he was engaged to be married, or why he then shot himself. The verdict returned by the jury was as follows:

We find that Mary Ann Yates met her death by the hand of James Brocklehurst Proctor, and that he maliciously, feloniously and of malice aforethought killed and murdered her. And we also find that James Brocklehurst Proctor wilfully committed suicide with malice aforethought.

The Fulwood Workhouse.

1851 Thomas and Catherine Murray were looking forward to an enjoyable evening watching a dog fight at the Wellington public house on Gartside Street, just off Deansgate Bolton. It was a good night and the ale flowed freely, until just after 10.30 p.m. when Thomas Murray answered the call of nature. While Thomas was out, Catherine got into an augment with one of the locals, a collier named 'Billy' Ball. The argument reached a climax when 'Billy' struck Catherine hard across the cheek. Thomas Murray, having returned and witnessed the attack **28 MAY**

on his wife, challenged Ball to go outside and settle the matter man to man. A large crowd gathered to witness the brawl. The throng began shouting and kicking at Murray, for, although he had the upper hand in the fight, he was doing little to hurt his opponent – and the crowd wanted blood. Among those kicking Murray was his own brother, 18-year-old Hugh Murray; another was Thomas Lord, and another who decided to join in was Patrick Regan. The kicking eventually became more and more violent, and Hugh Murray in particular aimed kick after kick at his brother's body with his hobnailed boots. Suddenly Thomas Murray lay on the ground motionless. The police soon arrived and everyone on the scene was arrested. Thomas Murray was taken home, but he never recovered and two days later he passed away. At the inquest it was decided that Hugh Murray should stand trial on a charge of manslaughter.

29 MAY   1847   James Lomax, of Great Harwood, ordered his keeper to take one of his lame otter hounds into the woods and shoot it. The keeper took the dog into the woods, tied up its legs and shot it, the bullet hitting it in the head. A week later Mr Lomax was passing through the wood and was alarmed to see the dog raise its head and bark. The keeper was sent for and was thunderstruck on seeing the animal. The poor creature was lying on the ground with its head resting on its forefeet – it was instantly shot. It appeared that the dog had survived the first bullet, as it had simply passed through the skin near its ear – the dog was stunned but not killed. It survived in that state for more than a fortnight, without food and enduring the cold night air.

30 MAY   1871   A vicious murder took place at Hambleton when an illegitimate son, Robert Hodgson, killed his mother, Jane Gardner. The incident occurred at about 12.30 in the early afternoon. Jane had been unwell for some time and was being sat with by two women when Robert Hodgson rushed into the room with a hatchet in his hand and struck his mother over the head, killing her on the spot. It appeared that mother and son had had frequent quarrels about the contents of Robert's late uncle's will, because all the money had been left to his mother. Hodgson was found guilty of wilful murder and was ordered to be tried at the next Lancaster Assizes. The jury here returned a verdict of 'guilty' with a recommendation for mercy – none was forthcoming from the judge however, and the death penalty was passed upon him. In late July the sentence was commuted to that of penal servitude for life.

31 MAY   1851   An inquest was held at the house of Miles Slaton, the New Inn in Goodshaw, on the body of 73-year-old John Hudson. It appeared that on

the previous Friday, at about seven o'clock, Hudson was crossing some fields near his house for the purpose of lighting a fire in Goodshaw Chapel. He had only gone a short distance when he fell down dead. A verdict of 'natural death' was recorded.

JUNE

The wrecked mill in Dean, damaged by an exploding steam engine. (*See* 26 June.)

1 JUNE **1867** Henry Farrington, who lived near Leigh railway station, had been married to his wife for about eighteen months; the union was not a happy one. The previous Monday, his wife had taken their child and gone to live with her uncle. The child, who was about 12 months old, was given to a nurse to enable the mother to work. On the following Thursday, Farrington took the child away from the nurse; when his wife went to his house that evening he threatened to shoot her. She escaped to the Rileys' house in the neighbouring village of Bedford, but had to leave the child behind. Finally, on Saturday night, Farrington asked Mrs Riley if she would ask his wife to return to him. His wife came to the door but

Henry Farrington shot his wife at point blank range – a crime for which he was later sentenced to death.

refused to go back with Farrington; she said that she wanted to take the child. Farrington said that he would never let her have the child – he would rather 'swing first'. He pulled out a pistol and shot his wife, killing her instantly. The murderer then fled down the lane towards the brook, dropping the pistol as he ran. He was seen by a passerby named Paul Stones, who followed and seized him near the brook before taking him to the police station, where he was charged with the murder. In August 1867, at the Farrington Assizes, he was sentenced to death for his crime.

2 JUNE **1578** Only Merseyside wit or sarcasm could result in calling a man over 9-ft tall the 'Child of Hale', but this was the name applied to John Middleton, the giant of a man born in 1578 at the quaint village of Hale in what is today Merseyside. A tree stump in the village, across from the church where he lies buried, can be seen today, carved into the shape of the giant. The inscription reads: 'Here lyeth the bodie of John Middleton, the Child of Hale, nine feet three.' A description of this enormous man was given in the *Liverpool Mercury* of 21 August 1840:

The tree stump which has been carved into the form of John Middleton.

In Brazenose College, Oxford ... his picture was taken, and now exists. A likeness of this English giant is also preserved at High Leigh, and one at Hale. His size is thus mentioned in Platt's 'History of Staffordshire': His hand from the 'corpus' to the end of his middle finger was 17 inches long, his palm 8 ½ inches broad, and his whole height 9 feet three inches – wanting but six inches of the height of Goliath, ... Some years ago when the late Mr Bushel was parish clerk and schoolmaster, the thigh bones were taken up from the earth, and were observed to reach from the hip of a man of common size to his foot. ... A descendant of his, Charles Chadwick, was living in 1804, and was above six feet high.

1894 There was a house fire at Rochdale. The cottage of Samuel Dean, 3 JUNE a core maker at 13 Back Crawford Street, was found to be on fire. At the time, four children were in the bedroom. Mrs Dean, who discovered the fire, gave the alarm, and Frank Austin and John M'Nichols rushed into the house with buckets of water and extinguished the flames. They rescued three of the children in an unconscious state, but the fourth, an infant, fell through the floor and was killed. Dr Wallace was soon in attendance, and the eldest child, aged 10, was brought round with some difficulty. Mrs Dean had left the house at 9.30 a.m., leaving the four children in bed. They had started playing with matches, which set fire to the bed clothes, and were soon overcome by the smoke. One of the children, aged 5, died from the effects of the smoke; a third later succumbed to the injuries he had received.

1886 A man named John Waite, a 34-year-old factory operative, went 4 JUNE into the local police station on Rochdale Road at Bacup and declared to PC Lowe that he had just murdered his wife. Waite was arrested; the officer went to his house and found the murdered woman 'weltering in gore'. On the floor, near her head, was a bread knife, and near her feet was a penknife – both were covered in blood. The walls, the furniture and the windows of the room were also covered in blood. There was utter chaos in the room itself – tables overturned, plant pots dislodged from the window sill and chairs scattered across the floor. Waite was later sentenced to death for the crime.

1869 Richard Riley, a rough-looking fellow, was brought before the 5 JUNE court at Colne and charged with an attempt to commit rape upon Aimee Widop, an 18-year-old who was residing with her parent at a farm near Foulridge. On the previous Friday, at about ten o'clock in the morning, the girl was making her way home from the village of Foulridge with a basket of provisions when, in a very lonely lane, some distance from her father's house, she was met by the prisoner. Without speaking, he threw her down. The poor girl screamed and struggled, and at last got up, upon which the prisoner threw her down for a second time. Once more she succeeded in getting up, but she was thrown to the ground for the third time. Eventually she escaped from her assailant and rushed home. She was much cut about the hands, wrists and knees from the struggle. From the description given to the police constable at Colne, Riley was suspected. He was apprehended soon afterwards, and identified by the girl as the person who had so violently assaulted her. PC Lord stated that he had visited the location of the assault, and it was evident that a violent struggle had taken place there. After a lengthy hearing, the prisoner was committed for trial.

6 JUNE   **1895**   Dr J. Sinclaire of Slaidburn was driving on the road near Dunsop Bridge at a good speed when the horse shied and the carriage overturned. The doctor was violently thrown out onto the road and sustained some serious injuries.

7 JUNE   **1878**   An underground explosion took place at the Wood Pit at Haydock; 189 men and boys perished. This is the official total, but other research has indicated that the total might have been even greater. The cause of the explosion was put down to a roof fall which ignited some firedamp (methane), which then tore through the workings. The youngest victim was just 12 years old. Nathan Boon lost his life and five of his sons in the disaster. This poem appeared soon after the explosion:

Weep Mothers, Weep o'er the loss of your dear ones,
The fathers and children who are strewn amongst the dead,
The explosion has filled the whole district with sadness,
For homes that are lonely, and hearts that have bled.

My Partner is gone, and my children are missing –
Sobs a heartbroken Mother in agony wild,
Great God, can it be we are parted forever?
Shall I never more see my dear husband and child?

T'was but early this morning, they left our own dwelling,
Me thought they seemed happy, contented and free;
How he'd spend his Whit week my poor boy was telling,
As he bound away with his innocent glee.

He oft joined with youthful companions,
In the hedges and lanes, he delighted to roam,

It seems strange to me, that my poor lad has perished,
Whilst his bosom companions are happy at home.

My dear husband kissed the sweet lips of the baby,
In sorrow I think of it now in the past,
He bade us as usual a hearty good morning,
Nor thought for a moment it would be his last.

Last words and last actions are ever enduring,
We seldom forget what our dear ones have said,
Their last words and deeds, we treasure with fondness,
We refer to them oft, when our loved ones are dead.

We miss each bright face in the family circle,
At their absence our hearts are bowed in despair;
We miss our dear child, when we see other children,
And we weep O'er a father as we look at his chair.

The place where they sat round the table is vacant,
Their friends and companions, they call to resign;
What prayers the dear mothers have breathed for their safety,
E''er the fathers and sons have descended the mine.

Though they are dead they still live in a mother's affection,
She prays, Oh Father look down on me
I trust you Thy Mercy in this hour of affliction,
For I read that though saved a thief on a tree.

Such conduct is worthy a wife and a mother,
Whose love and affection is ever the same,
She clings to her own where the heavens have darkened,
And she's faithful when enemies tarnished their flames.

This illustration shows the effects of the explosion at Wood Pit, as the crowds gathered waiting for news and the many dead were lain out to be identified by grieving wives and mothers.

There are sorrowing ones in the neighbourhood of Haydock,
God grant to them His help may be given,
Though the present be dark may Hope fill the bosom,
That at last they shall meet with their loved ones in Heaven.

Let us each give our mite in the cause of the widow,
To aid the poor orphans, there is room for each one;
If we give to the poor we lend to our Maker,
And to each willing helper He'll whisper, 'Well done'.

8 JUNE 1841 A fatal accident befell John Byrom, a mason employed at the Capernwray Quarry near Carnforth. He had blasted the rock when a fragment of stone unfortunately struck him on the head – he was precipitated down the quarry face a distance of 40 or 50 yards. John was so greatly injured that he died within three or four hours. An inquest on the body returned a verdict of 'accidental death'. The poor fellow was a member of the Mechanics' Club, and his remains were attended to the grave by a large body of members.

9 JUNE 1824 Pilling is a small village 6.5 miles from Poulton-le-Fylde in West Lancashire. To the east of the village stretches Pilling Moss, an expanse of peat bog. Here, for generations, the local folk had the rights of turbary – the right to dig the peat for fuel. Such was the case in June 1824, when a group of labourers were in a 6ft-deep peat pit digging the turf. One of the men became curious when his spade uncovered what appeared to be a piece of coarse yellow cloth. He pulled the cloth out of the ground to examine it, and was horrified to find that it was a human skull. It appeared to have been that of a female, having an abundance of beautiful auburn hair and a string of large black beads, held together with the first vertebrae of the neck. The hair was long and plaited; about 3in from the end of the braids it was cut off, as if by some heavy cutting instrument – not a single hair projected beyond. A short distance away was a house, used not many years previously as a receptacle, where females in a 'certain condition' were secretly conveyed. It was supposed at the time that the skull belonged to one of the unfortunate inmates, murdered by persons unknown. The rest of the body was never found.

10 JUNE 1888 Reports were emerging of a fatal fire at a newsagents in St Andrew's Street, Manchester, in which four lives were lost. The shop was kept by Martha Gains, and living on the premises were her 26-year-old son David, a 17-year-old servant girl named Mary Owens, and two lads, 14-year-old Thomas Owens, brother of the servant girl, and Charles Clegg, also aged 14. The fire broke out after they had all gone to bed.

FATAL FIRE IN MANCHESTER – FOUR LIVES LOST

The chaotic scene outside the burning shop in St Andrew's Street, where four people perished in 1888.

The two females occupied a room above the shop, the son stayed in an adjoining room, and the two lads were in an upper room. Mrs Gains was the first to become aware of the fire and she alerted the rest, who all rushed downstairs. Just at that moment, the windows and doors of the shop were shattered by the heat; the fresh air which then rushed up the stairway fuelled the fire further. There was no escape for the victims, and only David managed to save himself. The fire engines quickly arrived – but there were allegations that some of the firemen from outside Manchester had been attending a fireman's festival, were drunk and 'acted like madmen'. At one point a ladder was raised and a fireman went up to try and rescue those inside, but the ladder was removed and the fireman had to crawl along a ledge to save himself.

1894   Mary Ann Allen was separated from her husband; she ran a   11 JUNE
lodging house in Lomas Street, off Sandygate in Burnley, and took in washing to supplement her income. Also in the house lived her daughter Mrs Robinson, and the lodgers, William Crossley, Adam Robinson, Robert Chadwick and his two children. William Crossley worked at a foundry and also part time at the nearby Waterloo Hotel on Trafalgar Street. Crossley began to take an interest in Mrs Allen, but the relationship was not smooth and they were constantly arguing. Finally Crossley was told to move out of the house, and his bags were even packed for him on 11 June. At dinnertime he returned to the house while the family were sat around the table. Crossley said nothing, but went down to the cellar

Strangeways Prison, where William Crossley was hanged for the murder of Mary Ann Allen in 1894.

and brought back an axe. While Mrs Allen was drying her hands on a tea towel, he struck her across the back of her head. As he prepared to strike again, he was stopped by Robert Chadwick and Adam Robinson; her daughter also tried to intervene. In the mayhem, both Robinson and Mrs Allen's daughter received severe injuries to the head. In the confusion that followed, William Crossley simply walked out of the house and into the Waterloo Hotel, where he admitted to the landlord his terrible deed. The blow to Mrs Allen's head was fatal, and Crossley was soon taken into custody and charged with wilful murder. He was hanged for his crime at Strangeways Prison, Manchester.

12 JUNE   **1846**   At about 6.30, a heavy thunderstorm hit Little Lever and electric fluid struck the public house occupied by Joseph Little. It entered via a chimney, passed across a room and up another chimney. Although it had been in almost every corner of the house, no personal injury was sustained – but chairs were split, and it also broke several glasses and a clock.

13 JUNE   **1895**   At the police courts at Leigh, 16-year-old Charlotte Whitehouse of Robertshaw Street, Leigh was charged and committed to trial for the manslaughter of her 9-year-old brother Thomas William. Charlotte's mother and sister stated that when Charlotte had come home on Friday, her mother had beaten her with a sweeping brush, upon which the prisoner had kicked over a paraffin lamp. This had exploded and burnt her brother so badly that he died the following Saturday. The Bench thought

that it was a weak case, and in fact the Grand Jury at the Liverpool Assizes threw out the case in July that year.

1831 Samuel Hopkinson and his wife Mary, along with their friend Betty Partington, were strolling along the Manchester, Bolton & Bury Canal, returning from a funeral they had attended at Ringley Chapel. As they approached Fogg's Colliery on the canal, Betty said that she could do with a drink, and suggested that they stop off at the Farmers Arms, which was close by. Suddenly the trio were confronted by John McGowan, the night watchman at the colliery, who demanded to know what they were doing on the canal. McGowan was armed and, during the heated conversation that followed, Mary Hopkinson was shot by the man. McGowan ran off and a crowd quickly gathered at the scene, curious to know what the commotion was about. John McGowan returned to the scene a few minutes later and, to everyone's surprise, denied having shot Mary Hopkinson – even though he still had the gun in his hands with a bayonet fixed. Betty Partington was furious and challenged McGowan, but he replied that if she did not hold her tongue he would shoot her. With that he turned and strolled away into the darkness. Mary was removed to the Farmers Arms, but she died of her injuries three days later. McGowan was arrested and placed on trial at Lancaster Castle on Saturday, 13 August 1831. He was found guilty of killing Mary Hopkinson by firing a blunderbuss at her and was sentenced to be executed on 15 August. However, on the morning of the execution, his sentence was commuted to one of transportation for life. **14 JUNE**

1845 Eliza Montgomery was brought before the Bench at the Old Court House at Ashton-under-Lyne charged with having cruelly used a 14-month-old child. The prisoner had been out begging around the streets of Ashton, and had got so drunk that she was physically incapable of taking care of herself or her children. At this time she had three small children with her, one of which she threw down onto the pavement in Henry Square. The children were forcibly taken from her by women living in the neighbourhood, and Montgomery was arrested by police and taken to the lockup. The women who rescued the children were of the opinion that not all of them belonged to the accused. The chairman of the Bench had no difficulty in deciding what course to take with the prisoner – she would be jailed if not for the children. On the condition that she left town within half an hour, and did not return again, she was liberated. **15 JUNE**

1936 PC Crompton was on duty in the early hours when, at about 4.50 a.m., he heard screams and followed the sound to 12 Clitheroe Street, Padiham. Here he saw 40-year-old Arthur Roberts standing in a doorway **16 JUNE**

with a cut-throat razor in his hand – he was bleeding heavily from a deep wound across the front of his neck. Inside the property, the constable found his wife, Edith Alice Roberts, dead upon the floor with her throat cut. Roberts blurted out, 'I have done it, she was bothering with other men.' This statement was totally untrue, as proved later in court. Roberts collapsed upon the floor and the constable was obliged to give first aid until Dr Forsyth arrived a few minutes later. In the back bedroom a hammer was found on the bed, the bedclothes were saturated in blood and a trail led from the bedroom to the stairs, then downstairs where the deceased woman was found lying on the floor. Arthur Roberts was charged with the murder of his wife. In court, his 15-year-old daughter Florence broke down as she told how her mother met her death, and how she and her brother, 13-year-old Roy, had tried to protect her. Roy actually received a slight cut to his throat during the struggle, but his father said that this was not intentional. Even 8-year-old Norma, one of the younger daughters, was questioned.

'Did you see your daddy do anything when he got to the bottom of the stairs?' She was asked.

'Yes,' She replied, 'He cut his own throat.'

Mrs Roberts was laid to rest a few days later in Padiham church cemetery on Blackburn Road – members of the public were excluded by the gates, which were locked after the cortege had passed through. The mourners numbered just thirteen, and included three of the children, Florence, Roy and Norma, who was very badly affected by the proceedings. Arthur Roberts was later found guilty of the crime but judged to be insane.

17 JUNE **1870**   There was a boiler explosion at Messrs Cotton & Slater's Mill, King Street, Blackburn. The engine tenter was standing nearby and was forced some yards away through an 18in-thick wall. He was dreadfully scalded and killed on the spot. A young woman named Grogan and a young man named Shorrock were also killed. The sculleries and back kitchens of some of the adjoining houses were completely demolished and the whole neighbourhood shook as if in an earthquake. Five or six injured people were also removed to the infirmary.

18 JUNE **1887**   Reports of a murder committed in the Ancoats district of Manchester on 15 June were appearing in the local newspapers. James Dodd and Harriet Turner lived in a small house in Hadfield Street together with Dodd's seven children – all nine of them lived in one room in what must have been oppressive conditions. Early in the morning, the eldest son was awoken by the cries of one of the other children – he got out of bed and saw his father kneeling on Harriet, who was struggling to get away from him. As the lad got nearer, he saw that his father had a

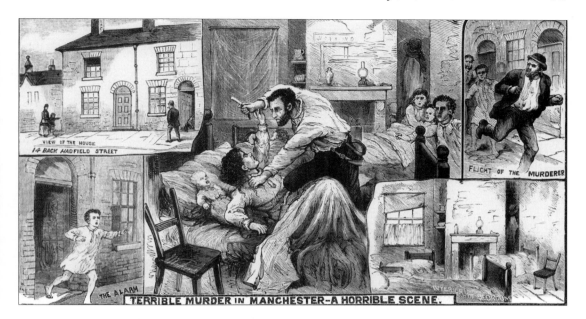

VIEW OF THE HOUSE / 14 BACK HADFIELD STREET

FLIGHT OF THE MURDERER

THE ALARM

INTERIOR OF BEDROOM

TERRIBLE MURDER IN MANCHESTER—A HORRIBLE SCENE.

razor in his hand and had inflicted a severe wound across the throat of the woman. The boy called out, but his father told him to be quiet or he would kill him. The boy jumped out of bed and ran into the street; his father followed him and, as they passed each other, he said, 'Goodbye son, you will never see me again.' The following day, Dodd's body was found floating in the canal. Verdicts of 'wilful murder' and 'suicide' were recorded at the inquest.

A depiction of the terrible scene in Hadfield Street, as James Dodd slits the throat of Harriet Turner whilst his children look on.

1885 Newspaper reports were being rushed out, giving details of a disaster which occurred the day before at the Clifton Hall Colliery on Lumns Lane. Around 200 men were below ground when the explosion tore through the workings of the pit – 178 of those men and boys would never again see daylight. Underground there was a supposed escape tunnel connecting the workings at Clifton Hall Pit with those of the Agecroft Colliery, but this was flooded with water almost to the very top, and, after the explosion, noxious gases hampered the rescue operations. The explosion happened in the Trencherbone Mine, and the ignition was caused by a lighted candle. A memorial to this disaster stands in St Augustine's Church on Bolton Road, where sixty-four of the victims were buried.

19 JUNE

1847 A cow belonging to a Mr Shaw of Trawden had a calf born with eight feet and two heads – but only two ears. It stood upon six legs, and had two distinct hind parts; both heads were very much alike. It was taken into the possession of John Simpson, bird stuffer at Colne, as every effort to deliver the calf in the natural way failed and her life was sacrificed.

20 JUNE

1817 Dean is a small hamlet near Waterfoot in the Rossendale Valley, a scattering of old cottages and farms. Sunny Field Farm here was occupied by William White in 1817. William had several children, but his pride and joy was his eldest daughter Ann who, with piercing dark blue eyes and rosy cheeks, was by far the loveliest girl in the Rossendale Valley. Ann was betrothed from her early teens to her childhood friend John Nuttall, who lived at the neighbouring farm three fields to the north at Harrow Stiles. However, the finger of scorn was pointed at Ann when it was discovered that she was to be a mother before she became a wife. Cold words and half-averted faces spread the gossip in this small rural community. To make matters worse, the very one to whom she had given so much was now showing resentment towards her. The gossip angered John Nuttall and, on the night of 21 June 1817, whilst the rest of the family slept, he headed for Sunny Field Farm. On arrival he tapped on the window of Ann's room, and she quickly joined him in the yard, wondering why he had come at such a late hour. John quietened her curiosity with a quick and gentle kiss and led her into the barn. Once inside, the old arguments raged, with John expressing his fury about the gossip around the village. 'Then marry me,' said Ann, but the angry exchanges continued. In a fit of temper, John grabbed hold of a fencing stake and struck poor Ann a fatal blow across her head – she gave a wide-eyed look of disbelief and, looking back at her lover, slumped lifeless to the ground. John thought of trying to hide the body, and carried her out

Sunny Field Farm in Dean, where Ann White was murdered by her lover John Nuttall. The barn where the killing took place is to the left of the farmhouse, with the arched door.

of the barn. It was, however, too much for him – the grief of his lost love was too much to bear and he placed her lifeless form in a well in the farmyard and fled the scene. No words can describe the feeling of Ann's parents who, as the sun rose that fine June day, found the dead body of their darling daughter half immersed in the still waters of the farmyard well. News quickly spread about the murder, for it was clear that was what it was, and soon it reached the Harrow Stiles household, who were sat in the kitchen having breakfast. The father asked John what he had been up to. John then jumped up and left the house. He wandered aimlessly over the moors, reaching the Deerplay Tool bar only to be sent on his way, for the toll bar keeper had heard the news. John was soon apprehended and committed to Lancaster Castle for trial. He was found guilty of murder and hanged for the offence. The funeral of poor Ann was held at St John's Church in Bacup, and was attended by hundreds of mourners. Later, an upright stone slab was placed over the unfortunate girl's final resting place, which was inscribed with the following words:

> In Memory of Ann, Daughter of William White
> Who Died 21 June 1817 in her 24th Year.
>
> Mourn Not For Me, When This You See
> Since God Was Pleased To Call Me
> I Was At Rest But Must Not Stay
> So My Poor Life Was Cast Away

Note: Following a published article that I wrote on this murder, Patricia Nuttall, who used to live at Sunny Field Farm, told the *Lancashire Evening Telegraph* that a relative of hers once saw Ann's ghost at the farm.

22 JUNE   1848   At Rochdale Petty Sessions, William Hartley of Brickfield, Small Bridge (a stout man aged about 30), was brought up on a charge of highway robbery. James Wrigley of Ridings stated that at about 12 o'clock on the previous Saturday evening, when returning home, two men had met him in Wardleworth Brow. They had knocked him down and rifled his pockets of £1 2s 6d in money and a silver watch. He had no doubt that the prisoner was one of the men. The prisoner was committed for trial at the next Assizes.

23 JUNE   1884   John Want, a collier from Burnley, and his wife had only been married six months – but it was not a happy marriage. Eventually John's wife left him and refused to return, but on 23 June 1884 he did persuade her to go for a walk. The walk took them past the Leeds & Liverpool Canal, and Want pushed his wife into the water. He then jumped into the water himself and pushed her away from the bank. Each time she came to the surface, he pushed her back under the water. While all this was going on, another collier named Shears arrived, attracted by the noise, and asked Want if anyone was drowning. Want replied, 'It's only my mate who has fallen in the water, I can get him out myself.' At that moment, Shears saw the woman come to the surface, and Want once again pushed her under. Shears ran down to the water's edge and rescued the woman. For trying to drown his wife, John Want was later sentenced to 20 years' imprisonment.

1847   An inquest was held at the Black Swan Inn, Greenacres Moor,   24 JUNE Oldham to investigate the circumstances attending the death of a woman named Travis, the wife of a cotton mill workman living at Rhodes Field. It appeared that two days previous, the woman had been seized with the pains of labour. Her husband, at the request of his wife, asked for the assistance of a surgeon resident in the district, but that gentleman was otherwise engaged and the surgeon asked that the husband might apply for assistance elsewhere. The husband, however, stubbornly refused, and continued to loiter around the surgery for a considerable time. In the meantime, his wife became considerably worse. The jury at the inquest did not attach any blame to the medical gentleman, but the husband, who was upwards of 30 years of age, was censured for his conduct in not seeking medical assistance elsewhere. The jury returned a verdict of 'death from natural causes'.

The Black Swan Inn, where the inquest was held on a woman who might have survived had her husband gone for alternative medical help.

25 JUNE   **1862**   Enoch Feather was charged with killing David Moory in The Queens public house at Bacup. Feather was worse for drink and had picked an argument with a number of customers in the pub. Finally there was only Feather, David Moory and Jonas Boothman left in the inn. There was a heated exchange between Feather and Moory, and Feather strolled across the room and struck Moory a single blow across the face – Moory immediately expired. Enoch Feather was charged with manslaughter. Medical evidence showed that Moory had extensive clotting on the brain caused by external violence. The jury at the inquest returned a verdict of 'guilty' with a recommendation for mercy. The prisoner was then sentenced to two months' imprisonment with hard labour.

The Queens public house, where Enoch Feather extinguished the life of David Moory in June 1862.

26 JUNE   **1858**   The steam engine was the great muscle of the Industrial Revolution, powered by large boilers producing immense pressures of steam – but these boilers had an alarming tendency to explode through too much pressure. Such was the case of the boiler explosion at the Dean Mill, or Spring Mill, at Dean in Rossendale, by which Hannah Howarth, Thomas Nuttall and Hargreaves Lord perished. The mill was only built in 1853 and the blast was so great that it propelled the boiler from its bed and sent it in two different directions, one part landing a great distance away. The coroner's inquest recorded a verdict of 'accidental death' in each case, expressing at the same time a conviction that the boiler blew as a consequence of over pressure, and suggesting that there had been want on the part of the engineer and members of the firm for which they ought to be reprimanded.

1858 Another disastrous boiler explosion took place at the weaving shed belonging to Messrs Holden Crothers at Daisyfield, Blackburn, which resulted in the instant death of the engine tenter Henry Seed. The boiler was fixed against the end of the shed with its back end against the chimney. Parallel with the boiler, and separated from the boiler house by a road about 20ft wide, were three cottages; the deceased lived in the middle one. The explosive force against the chimney caused about 20-30ft of it to topple to the ground and mingle with the ruins of the boiler house. The unfortunate Henry Seed was standing at the boiler house door, looking towards the cottages, when the explosion forced his body upon the threshold of his own door. Hot coal was scattered towards the cottages – several windows were broken and the clothes of the deceased's wife caught fire. The flames were soon extinguished and she did not come to too much harm.

The wreckage and destruction caused by the massive boiler explosion at Dean Mill in June 1858.

28 JUNE **1890** Edward Young, a joiner, went to the district police station at Manchester and told officers that he had just killed his wife. At the same time, two of his eight children ran to his wife's sister's house and told her, 'Daddy has killed mummy and the baby.' The police found the woman lying on the bed at the very point of death – she was horribly

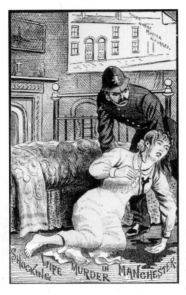

gashed on the neck and breast, the wound having been inflicted by a table knife. She expired within a few minutes. The baby was safe, although splattered with its mother's blood. The murder was apparently committed because the wife objected to the husband smoking in bed. Evidence at the inquest heard how Young was often unkind to his wife, and in fact had been in prison for stabbing her just nine weeks earlier. The jury returned a verdict of 'wilful murder' against Edward Young and he was committed to trial. In spite of a plea that the prisoner was insane, the courts sentenced him to death by hanging in July 1890.

Edward Young's wife lay dying on the floor of the bedroom where he had cut her throat and breast.

29 JUNE **1876** There was great amusement at Southport when the town was enlivened by a street pantomime. It appeared that a gentleman who

was well known in the locality had offended the larger population of the town. An effigy of the man concerned was placed on the back of a donkey and transported through the streets, preceded by a brass band playing 'The Rogue's March'. At nine o'clock the figure was suspended from a makeshift gallows near the pier, and was afterwards cut down and burnt to ashes to the laughter and cheers of thousands of people.

A scene of great amusement in Southport.

30 JUNE **1852** An inquest was held at the Pineapple public house in Darcy Lever, Bolton touching on the death of 9-year-old John Halliwell, who fell into the water lodge belonging to William Gray, the Mayor of Bolton. A verdict of 'accidental death' was recorded.

JULY

How the *Illustrated Police News* depicted the murder of Elizabeth Brindle by James Hamer, who later hanged himself. (*See* 23 July.)

1 JULY **1869** An inquest was held at the Fisherman's Inn, Hollingworth Lake, Littleborough, on the deaths of 23-year-old Mary Ann Holt and 24-year-old Ellen Brooks, both of York Street, Todmorden. The previous Monday night, the women had been on a drive round the lake when they stopped at the toll bar to pay the toll. Without warning, their horse backed into the lake, there being no wall or proper embankment there. The jury returned a verdict that the women met their deaths by accident, adding that the lake was in an unprotected and dangerous state.

2 JULY **1845** Four-year-old John Thomas, of Wilton Street, Heywood, went with his mother for steam water in the factory yard of John Hilton Kay & Sons. In the yard there was a revolving shafting which ran from the cotton mill to the shed. It was about 12in above the ground, and persons going for the steam water had to stride over it. The unfortunate youngster was climbing over the shafting when his pinafore and frock caught hold, and the boy was turned round at least thirty times. His head was so injured that he died fifteen minutes later. An inquest was held on the body at the Brunswick Hotel before T.H. Dearden. It appeared from the evidence of several witnesses that the tub containing the steam water was placed in the yard of the mill by the management for the use of their workers. One of the jurymen observed that a piece of lead piping valued at about 2*s* might convey the water so that a person would not have to cross over the shafting. The coroner ordered that no person should be allowed to fetch water from that place until the shafting had been boxed in, or a pipe had been laid to convey the steam water to a safe place. The jury then returned a verdict of 'accidental death'. A few weeks previous, a woman's dress had caught in a similar manner, but luckily the trapped piece tore off, or she would have met a similar death.

3 JULY **1837** Elizabeth 'Betty' Read, aged 69, was charged with the murder of George Burgess at Waddington village near Clitheroe. When Elizabeth's husband opened the cottage door, he gave a cry at the dreadful spectacle which presented itself, and stepped back out onto the street. A neighbour's young son was lying on his back upon the floor; he was surrounded by blood and his brains protruded from a large gash on his tiny skull. Blood was traced back into another room, from where the deceased infant had been dragged. An axe was later found on the floor of the cottage, stained with blood and with portions of hair and the fleshy parts of the brain adhering to it. A bent poker was also found, and in the back room the floor and walls were sprinkled with blood and brain matter. On being questioned, the prisoner admitted the offence, and said that she had been ordered to do so seven years ago by Jesus Christ. It came out in evidence that the prisoner was not in her right mind, and that the parish officers

had previously tried to get her removed to the asylum – they were only prevented from doing so by her husband wishing her to remain at home, 'She being very harmless and he being willing to take care of her.' Mr James Garstang, a surgeon, proved that the prisoner was insane. The jury found the prisoner 'not guilty' on the grounds of insanity.

1852 Rawtenstall weaver, James Reddyhough, was rather drunk, **4 JULY** having spent the night drinking beer in Rochdale. He started walking home to Rawtenstall, but decided that it was too far and the night might be better spent at the house of his father-in-law at Oak Street. The streets were dark and quiet in these early hours, and James soon got lost. Eventually he spotted another person, and approached him to ask for directions. The man led him into Manchester Road – the opposite direction to which James should have been going. Getting some distance beyond the houses, the man attacked Reddyhough, knocking him to the ground – blood gushed from his mouth. While down, his assailant rifled his pockets, taking two half crowns and a bottle of rum before running off. Reddyhough tried to give chase, but was hampered by his injuries and drunken condition. A man named John Marcroft had seen the incident; he came to Reddyhough's aid and managed to get him to his father-in-law's house. Marcroft was able to give the police a description of the robber, and about two hours later they tracked him down – he was at that time in a state of intoxication. His name was Joseph Brown, a cotton weaver from Scotland. At the magistrates' court he denied all knowledge of the robbery, but Reddyhough and Marcroft identified him and he was committed for trial at the Salford Sessions.

1844 A fatal accident occurred at Pigslee Bridge near Ramsbottom. **5 JULY** At about three o'clock, a man named John Spencer was on the bridge in conversation with Mrs Heys, the wife of a shopkeeper in Fletcher Bank, when a cart laden with timber came very rapidly down the brow. It was thrown over directly opposite where they were standing, killing Mrs Heys and breaking Spencer's leg. Mr Parks, a surgeon, was soon in attendance, and did all he could to alleviate Spencer's suffering. The cart was the property of John Parkinson of Ewood Bridge, near Haslingden, and was driven by John Clegg, who had done everything in his power to stop the horses. The deceased left five children. An inquest was held at the New Inn, Walmsley, where a verdict of 'accidental death' was returned. The jury expressed a hope that this accident would make carters more attentive in their duties.

1864 A piece of coal fell from the basket being drawn up the pit shaft of **6 JULY** the coal mine belonging to Mr Case at Woodhouses, Bardsley. It struck a woman at the shaft bottom named Jane Gore. She was so badly injured that she died within three days; an inquest was held on the body and a verdict of 'accidental death' was returned.

7 JULY 1849 The *Manchester Guardian* reported on the body of a 7-week-old child, which was discovered in a cesspool under strange circumstances at Bedford, near Leigh in South Lancashire. The body was found by furniture broker Mr Unsworth, and recognised as being the child of John Parkinson. The mother was apprehended shortly afterwards and taken to the police station at Leigh. It was stated that the mother had been drinking for the previous two days and had not been sober during that time. She had been seen with the child at the Shoulder of Mutton public house on the previous Friday, but later that afternoon she claimed that she had lost it. When the child was found by Mr Unsworth, it had a portion of its head and one of its arms immersed, and a handkerchief tied around its head – but in such a way that it did not cover its mouth. An inquest into the child's death was expected to be held later in the week.

8 JULY 1837 At the Preston Sessions, William Robinson was charged with stealing a pair of shoes and a waistcoat at Winmarleigh Old Hall (near Garstang) and was sentenced to be transported for seven years.

9 JULY 1899 Martin Tighe, a 54-year-old miner from Wigan, objected when his wife brought alcohol into their house; an argument and a struggle followed. This continued until about seven o'clock at night, when their young daughter was sent to buy oatmeal at the local shop. The shop was only a few hundred yards away and she was back in the house within a few minutes. However, she found that the kitchen door was locked and, after knocking for a few minutes and getting no answer, she kicked one of the panels out. Her father then let her in, and the girl saw her mother on the kitchen floor in a pool of blood. All her father could say was, 'I have done it. I have done it'. At his trial in August, Martin Tighe was sentenced to death.

10 JULY 1864 James Wood and his wife Annie were brought before the magistrates at Wigan on a charge of riotous and disorderly conduct in the market place on the previous Tuesday. From police evidence it appeared that the defendants were fighting; the woman had been exceedingly noisy and was taken into custody at once. Her husband was shortly afterwards 'lodged' in the lockup. Wood and his wife had frequently been guilty of similar offences while intoxicated. On this occasion, it appeared that the wife was the aggressor; she was accordingly sentenced to a month's imprisonment, and her husband was discharged.

1850   Mr Charles Juckes, a surgeon of Cheetham Hill, Manchester was 11 JULY
charged with evading the toll at the White Smithy Bar at Crumpsall. He
rode through Wilton Polygon and got on the Middleton Road without
passing through the toll bar. Mr Juckes, in answer to the charge, stated
that he had had to call upon a patient at Polygon, and afterwards
had to go to Blackley, so he went through Polygon instead of turning
back into the road and round by the bar. The case was dismissed on
account of Mr Juckes paying costs and the amount of money due in
tolls. Mrs Richardson, the owner of the land in Wilton Polygon, was
then summoned for allowing the road through Polygon to be used for
the purpose of evading tolls. Her son appeared and stated that she was
obliged by her lease of the land from the Earl of Wilton to leave the road
open – the case was then dismissed.

1850   An inquest was held at the house of Thomas Dean, Old Cross Inn, 12 JULY
Radcliffe Hall near Bury on the death of 2-year-old Betty Smith. Margaret
Smith, the child's mother, went out of the house to feed the pigs and,
having lifted up the lid of the swill tub, she heard her 7-week-old infant
crying in its cradle. She returned to the house to see what the matter was.
Betty went over to the swill tub, which was sunk into the ground so that
the top of it was only half a yard high. She fell into the tub and drowned,
and was found later by a neighbour. The mother was greatly affected by
the accident and had to be removed from the property. The father of the
child was criticised, at the request of the jury, for not securing the tub
better against accidents; he promised to increase the height above ground
in the future. A verdict of 'accidental death' was recorded.

The Old Cross Inn,
where the inquest
was held on the
body of Betty Smith.
(Jack Nadin)

13 JULY 1849 An inquest was held at the Old Bay Horse Inn, Cooper Street, Bury touching on the death of 31-year-old David Bates, a coach trimmer in the employ of Burrows & M'Call coach builders. Bates had expired on the Friday evening previous, while fighting in front of the Old Bay Horse with a person named Matthew Wood. Witnesses testified that Wood struck Bates in the pit of the stomach, after which he fell to the pavement and died. The jury returned a verdict of 'died through excitement while in a state of intoxication'.

14 JULY 1831 At Blackburn Petty Sessions, Henry Occleshaw of Walton-le-Dale, an inn keeper, was fined £5 and costs for permitting a bear to be baited on his premises. It appeared from the evidence brought forward that nearly 300 people had assembled at his house to witness the brutal exhibition.

15 JULY 1854 There was a terrible boiler explosion at the Bridgefield Mill at Oakenrod, Rochdale worked by George Williamson. The night before the accident, the boiler attendant was drunk and was taken into custody by the police; his place was taken by Howarth, manager of the mill, and a person named William Taylor. They proceeded to get up steam, when suddenly the boiler blew up in a massive explosion. Most of the factory was obliterated and a cottage occupied by Howarth was destroyed – and with it his wife. Her father and two of the children were in bed at the time and the bed, the mattress and the occupants were blown into the river, but amazingly they all survived. A nearby cotton mill belonging to Mr Bottomley received a broadside of bricks and metal, which entered the mill through the windows and travelled the full length of the building. A young woman was struck by a brick and killed; the head of another young woman was found near her, the remainder of the poor creature lay under the rubble. In total, ten people perished in the boiler explosion, although inital reports only listed nine fatally wounded: Ann Stott, a weaver aged 22 years; Ann Nicholson, aged 21, a weaver; Joseph Greenwood, a young jobber; Thomas Howarth, the 37-year-old overlooker and manager; Sarah Howarth, his wife, aged 35; William Taylor, an overlooker aged about 40; Betsy Brierley, aged 20, a weaver; Alice Ashworth, 21, a weaver; and Jane Halkyard, a young weaver. Scores of others were injured to some extent.

The scene following a boiler explosion like the one at Bridgefield Mill, and the devastation left behind.

1961 Seven people were killed (the driver and six passengers) and 116 were injured when two trains collided at about 45 miles per hour near Weeton, Lancashire. The 8.50 diesel multiple unit train from Colne to Fleetwood crashed into the rear of a ballast train, which had been working in the vicinity of Singleton Bank signal box. The signalman at Singleton misunderstood a telephone message, which led him to make a serious error and accept the diesel train irregularly. The accident report also strongly criticised the local inspectors for allowing poor working practices.

1852 There was a boiler explosion at the Armriding Mill at Euxton, near Chorley. The three-storey mill stood on the banks of the river Jarrow and was worked by a steam engine of 12hp and a water wheel of 15hp, which took water from the river. The explosion killed two men, William Calderbank and William Dickson.

1859 At Blackrod, a 40-year-old man named Joseph France was drowned in a coal pit as a consequence of a storm. Joseph France and Clarkson Bullough were employed in sinking a shaft at Brinks Colliery, belonging to the Earl of Balcarres. At seven o'clock they came up for refreshment during a storm, and, when the storm appeared to be abating, they were let down again by the engine to resume their work. The rain, however, continued to fall in torrents, and came down from the hills in such a body as to extinguish the engine fire, and to fill the bottom of the shaft to a depth of 20 yards. The man who had charge of the engine was unable to draw up France or his companion, so he let down a rope to help them keep themselves above the water until the engine fire could be renewed. Bullough, who was swimming upon a plank, got hold of the rope and was saved – but France failed to do so and drowned. An inquest was held later at the Red Lion Inn, the verdict being 'accidental death'.

1863 An inquest was held touching the death of Oliver Hatch, a quarryman at Scorton. Hatch was ascending the windlass when the barrow overturned; he was precipitated to the bottom of the quarry and received injuries from which he later died.

1832 An inquest was held at Brindle on the body of a child discovered in extraordinary circumstances. John Alston was bringing in some cows from a field when he saw something 2 or 3 yards from the path – he thought it was a dead lamb. However, when he touched it he found it was a dead child, and gave the information to the police.

On the previous Tuesday, John Parker had gone into the outhouse where his mother lived and, in one corner of the room, had seen something which he took to be a Boggart. He brought it downstairs and laid it on the grass near the midden. Later in the day he went to see it and found that it was gone. On Saturday night he went again, and found it near the area where he had first placed it; he picked it up and threw it over the hedge into an adjoining field.

The surgeon who examined the body stated that the child was fully grown and had nails, and hair upon its head – though it appeared to have been dead for over twelve months. He also said that on 11 January 1831, he had been called to examine a female named Jenny Critchley of Brindle, to see if she was with child. She had denied it, although he believed she was in an advanced state of pregnancy. Mary Parker, who lived next door to the Critchleys, had noticed that Jenny was with child. Other witnesses were called, whose statements supported the theory that the child was Jenny Critchley's – although that particular point was not pursued any further. In the end, the rather remarkable verdict of the jury was 'Found dead, but it does not appear whether it was born alive'.

21 JULY 1905 There was a terrible rail crash at the Hall Road Station on the Lancashire & Yorkshire Railway between Bootle and Formby, to the north of Liverpool. The 16.30 express train – one of the few electric trains in operation at that time – was running from Liverpool Exchange to Southport; it collided with a local train which had departed from Liverpool ten minutes earlier and was being turned round at Hall

Hall Road Station, where the fatal accident occurred in 1905.

Road Station. The local train had been shunted into a siding to allow the express to pass. Whether the points had been closed afterwards, or whether the express had jumped the rails, was never discovered. Twenty-one people were killed and up to forty-five were injured, many seriously. Amazingly, the local train driver escaped injury.

1849 Wigan coal miner, Henry Critchley, had volunteered to be lowered down an old coal pit at Hardybutts, known as Mr Lowe's Pit, for the purpose of examining the workings in order to investigate any damage that might have incurred to nearby property through subsidence. He descended the shaft with a safety lamp in hand; on reaching the bottom, he found that the pit was dry and he was able to traverse several of the passages – until he was stopped by bad air. He made a second attempt later in the afternoon, and, as he approached the pit bottom for the second time, he was alarmed to see a dog spring across the shaft above him. Thinking that this was some phantom of the dark, Critchley grabbed a large stone to 'dash out the animal's brains'. But when he raised the stone, the animal backed off, as if in a plea for mercy. On being lowered to the bottom, 'Poor Fanny' – for that proved to be her name – leapt about in sheer delight, and began licking her saviour excitedly. On being raised to the top of the pit she leaped out onto *terra firma*, delighted at having been saved from the dark depths. How did she come to be there? It appeared that around 30 April previous, there was a dispute between a local mother and her son about the upkeep of the animal. The boy, in a fit of anger, flung Poor Fan down the shaft, which reached a depth of around 300ft. At the time of Poor Fan's rescue, she had been in the pit about twelve or thirteen weeks – how the poor creature escaped death from the fall, or how she managed to sustain life, was never discovered. However, Fanny was taken into the care of John Farrington, a broker in the town, and seemed none the worse for her alarming experience.

22 JULY

1868 Young Elizabeth Brindle, the daughter of John Brindle of Shuttling Field Farm, near Higher Walton, had been courting her childhood sweetheart, James Hamer, for many years. They both worked at Mr Bourne's Brindle Mill not far away. A few weeks previously, Elizabeth had argued with her lover about his habits of smoking and chewing tobacco and asked him to stop, as they were saving up. James objected, and after a raging row the couple separated. On Wednesday 23 July, Elizabeth received a note from James Hamer asking her to meet him in a place called John Martin's Field, not far from her house. Elizabeth saw no objection to this and assumed that James wanted to make up. She left the mill with her sister at around 6.30 p.m. on that warm summer's

23 JULY

Alma Row, where James Hamer was last seen alive after murdering his sweetheart.

evening; as she approached the named place Hamer came into view, and the sister left them to it. Half an hour later, a man named James Yates was walking along Alma Row when Hamer passed him at great speed with a piece of rope in his hand. A few yards further along the lane, Yates was horrified to find Miss Brindle slumped by a gate with a gaping wound across her throat – the ground around her was saturated with her blood. As Yates tried to comfort her, she cried out, 'Oh, Jim, James Hamer has done this to me, because I told him I would not go with him. I wish my punishment was over.' The alarm was given, but by the time the surgeon, Mr Spencer, arrived at the scene, poor Elizabeth Brindle had died. Two and a half hours later, a spinner at Brindle Mill found James Hamer in a field suspended from a tree by a rope – he too was dead. Later the courts gave a verdict of 'wilful murder' against Hamer for taking the life of Elizabeth Brindle, and a verdict of 'suicide' against himself.

24 JULY   1850   At the Rochdale Sessions, George Stott, William Kay and John Kershaw, who all said that they were dyers from Halifax, were charged with being drunk and disorderly in a railway carriage. It appeared from the evidence of Mary Ann Houldsworth, and others, that the prisoners had left Manchester on Tuesday evening by the 7.30 train. They had a jar of whisky, which they served round to the company. The witness, Houldsworth, refused the offer and the prisoners used very abusive language towards her, and to the others who refused to drink with them. On arrival at the Blue Pits Station she complained to the inspector, but he took no action. The defendants continued to drink and make a nuisance of themselves until disembarking at Rochdale Station. Here, David Fletcher, an inspector, took them into custody and placed them in the lockup. They were all fined 5s and 15s 6d costs; this was paid and the men were released.

1889   Twenty-three-year-old Walter Davies managed the pawnbroker's
shop for John Lowe on Market Street at Atherton. On this day, as usual,
he went to the shop at around 7 a.m. and started to 'dress' the window
displays, placing watches and other valuables in full view of the passing
public. Just before nine o'clock, a man came into the shop to pawn a
silk handkerchief. A passer-by remarked on seeing Davies behind the
counter a few minutes later. Ten minutes after this, some children were
playing outside the shop and one of them – a lad named Clewes – peered
in through the open cellar window and saw Davies lying in a pool of
blood. The lad ran off to tell his parents. Mr Clewes returned with the
lad and, finding that the account was true, informed the owner of the
shop, Mr Lowe. Both gentlemen went down the cellar steps, Mr Lowe
picking the young man up by the shoulders to check his condition –
as he did so, the man gave out a low sob and expired. A few months
later, a man named John Edward Lorn was charged on suspicion of the
murder when he tried to pawn some watches, but this charge was later
reduced to one of robbery. A man named William Chadwick was then
charged, and after a prolonged length of time was brought before the
judges at the Assizes; in March 1890 the death sentence was passed
upon him. The prisoner, on hearing the verdict, turned to his wife and
simply exclaimed, 'Goodbye, Polly, goodbye.' He protested his innocence
to the very last, but on Tuesday, 15 April 1890, William Chadwick was
hanged at Kirkdale Prison, Liverpool.

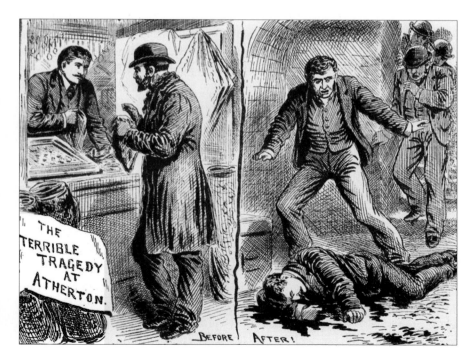

The murder at the
pawnbroker's in
Atherton in 1889.

26 JULY **1885** On two occasions, Mr Robert Whitaker of Royton, a cotton spinner, manufacturer and county magistrate, had been before the Manchester magistrates on a charge of perjury in connection with the purchase of some mills, and the sale thereof to a public company. A civil action arising out of the same transaction was also down for a hearing at the Manchester Assizes.

When the case was called on, it was announced that Mr Whitaker had committed suicide. He had woken up at about eight o'clock and cut his throat, dying in about an hour. He was 65 years of age, a prominent figure in the Oldham spinning trade, and was the chairman of the Royton Bench of Magistrates. The prosecutor in the charge of perjury was the deceased's own son.

Mr Robert Whitaker, a well respected man, committed suicide in 1885.

27 JULY **1848** A building in West Street at Bent, near Oldham was discovered to be on fire. It was used by four or five individuals for making cotton waste. As soon as the fire was discovered the alarm was given, and the West of England fire engine was on the spot, quickly followed by the town's engine. The fire spread rapidly and soon the whole building was enveloped in flames. Only a small portion of the waste could be saved, and the efforts of the firemen turned towards the engine house, which they succeeded in saving. The damage amounted to around £300, but the buildings were insured. The jealousy which had long existed between the men belonging to the different engines was allowed to prevail to such an extent that they commenced quarrelling on arrival, pumping water on each other instead of directing their efforts to the flames.

28 JULY **1827** The appalling murder of a 6-year-old took place near Rochdale. The crime was committed by woollen weaver Henry Howorth, who cut the throat of William Worral for no apparent reason. The deceased had gone to Howorth's to play, and was sitting in a chair when Howorth approached him with a razor and inflicted such severe wounds upon the child's throat that he died instantly. Howorth then cut his own throat, but several people arrived and prevented him from dying. An inquest on the child recorded a verdict of 'wilful murder' against Henry Howorth, who was committed to the next Lancaster Assizes for trial. Howorth was later found to be insane, and was ordered to be detained at the pleasure of the Crown.

1850   At Bury police station, James Hardman, a weaver of Walmsley-cum-Shuttleworth, was charged with assaulting Jonathan Taylor. The latter had been in the tap room of the Red Lion Inn, Bolton Street, Bury, when Hardman took hold of him and threw him against the fender. He bled about the head and had to have medical attention – he had done nothing to provoke Hardman whatsoever. The defendant pleaded that he was intoxicated at the time. He was fined 20*s* and costs, or seven days at the Salford house of correction.   29 JULY

1850   Several men were engaged in erecting scaffolding at a house on Cheetham Hill Road, just beyond the Temple toll bar. Two of the men, Gralton and Salmon, were standing on a plank, stooping to reach down for another, when the plank gave way and Gralton fell backwards over a wall and down some cellar steps. Salmon staggered considerably but managed to save himself. When other workmen went to Gralton's assistance, they found his eyes hanging from their sockets and blood gushing from his mouth and ears. One of the men jumped into a cab and got medical assistance, but the man died before he returned. The surgeon said that his skull was fractured. An inquest was held later at the Eagle & Child, Cheetham Hill where a verdict of 'accidental death' was recorded.   30 JULY

1883   Elizabeth Moore was charged with bigamy at the Liverpool Assizes, having married John Cousins at Burnley on 2 June 1883, whilst her first husband was still alive. The prisoner pleaded guilty to the charge, and her defence – in a very effective speech – detailed her former life with her husband. He had deserted her on a number of occasions and starved her. Two of their children had actually died from privation. He had also brutally assaulted her several times, wounding her about the head and the body. They had been parted about four years when she married again. The prisoner was of good character, sober and honest. She was ordered to be imprisoned for one week with hard labour.   31 JULY

AUGUST

The memorial erected by American servicemen to the memory of those who perished in the Freckleton air disaster. (*See* 23 August.) (Jack Nadin)

1 AUGUST 1872 A collision, which caused serious loss of life and considerable damage to the rolling stock, occurred on the Lancashire & Yorkshire Railway near Pendleton, Manchester. The 11.30 express, running from Manchester Victoria Station, was timed to stop at Pendleton Station at 11.38. The train arrived at Pendleton safely, and, after picking up some passengers, continued on to the next stop at Moses Gate. About a mile further up the line, at a place near Messrs Andrew Knowles & Co.'s colliery siding at Agecroft, the driver of the express was under the impression that the signals showing ahead indicated that the line was clear. As the engine of the express was passing over the points where the coal sidings joined the main line, a heavily-laden coal train connected with the main line. The tender of the coal train was hit by the left buffer of the express train, throwing both engines off the rails, followed by the express train carriages. The aftermath of the crash was four dead and many injured. Those killed were 34-year-old William Hilton of Preston, 33-year-old Emma Crossley, 54-year-old John Winward, and 43-year-old Thomas Holmes.

2 AUGUST 1848 At the petty sessions, Laurence Longworth, George Rawlinson, and William Walsh of Guide, Lower Darwen were charged with setting fire to a shippon. Jacob Hoghten stated that his shippon had burnt down on 18 July, and only a small part of the door remained. John Hunt, a labourer, said that he was drinking with the defendants below a haystack on the afternoon of 18 July. He left them for a time, and when he saw them next they were climbing over the wall of the yard in which the shippon stood. No one else was nearby. The case was adjourned in order for the complainant to bring forward further evidence.

3 AUGUST 1881 The year was 1879, and 14-year-old Annie Ratcliffe, the landlord's daughter at the Blue Bell Inn, Preston had attracted the attention of John Aspinall Simpson, a 19-year-old local lad. Simpson was a clerk by profession, but most of the time he was out of work and spent his days gambling and drinking. Annie's father, Alf, was fully aware of what was going on, and quite naturally objected to the affair – not only because of the age difference, but also because he had an acute dislike for Simpson. Simpson was barred from the pub and told that under no circumstances was he ever to see Annie again. The couple carried on meeting though, and by the time Annie was 16 she was pregnant. Reluctantly, Annie's father signed the consent form for the couple to wed, insisting that he would not be going to the wedding, nor would Simpson ever be welcome in his house. Simpson looked a little unsure of what was happening, and was seemingly having second thoughts. The wedding was planned for 1 August, but Simpson made an excuse that the marriage had to be put off until the following Wednesday, 3 August. The couple then met at the Sir Walter Scott pub on North Road, and withdrew to a small side room at the inn. A few minutes later the landlady heard shouts, and rushing into the room found Annie staggering across the bar with a gaping wound across her throat. Simpson sat motionless at a table with a bloodstained razor at his side. Simpson later claimed insanity, but the judge still found him guilty of murder – a crime for which he was hanged at Strangeways Prison on 28 November 1881. The following pitiful words were on the bottom of a memorial card printed in memory of young Annie Ratcliffe:

Inside the Sir Walter Scott, where John Aspinall Simpson brutally slashed the throat of his lover Annie Ratcliffe in 1881.

> That lovely morn I fully hoped should I become a wife
> And had no fear that one so dear would take away my life
> But death doth come in many forms, though painful was my lot
> I pray for those I've left behind, and say 'Forget me Not'

1852 A boiler exploded at the Pitfield Mill at Bamford, about 2 miles from Rochdale, killing four people and injuring several others. The mill was being worked by Bearon & Tattersall, manufacturers, who had attached a two-storey-high boiler house. The upper floor was being used as a lumber room and contained two self-acting mules. There were three boilers in the room below, and, at the time of the accident, two of them were driving an engine of about 30hp. One of the boilers was nearly new, but the other was said to have been in use for sixteen years or more, and had been repaired many times. At 6.45 a.m. the boiler burst completely, destroying the boiler house and a number of outbuildings. There were three people in the room above the boilers, and when they were dug out of the rubble two of them were dead, and the third so badly injured that he died later that morning. The assistant engineer, who happened to be passing the boiler room at the time, was also instantly killed. Those killed were James Kershaw, 24, John Shepherd, 26, James Kershaw, 14, and Alice Standring, aged 13.

4 AUGUST

1873 Andrew Mullany, 34, was charged at the Salford Summer Assizes for wounding Bartley Towers, a sergeant in the county police force. The prisoner and his wife lodged in a house in Canal Street, Openshaw and on 24 June they were quarrelling about a four penny piece. Mullany left, not intending to return – but at ten o'clock that night he came back,

5 AUGUST

and Mrs Davies, the landlady, would not let him in as he was drunk. He did, however, succeed in getting into the house, and Mrs Davies sent for the police. It was while he was in custody that the assault took place. As Towers was taking his charge down to the cells, he dropped his pen, and was stooping to pick it up when the prisoner kicked him violently in the groin. A scuffle took place that lasted twenty minutes, but the officer succeeded in getting the man locked up. When Towers received medical treatment the following day, it was found that he had an extensive rupture of the groin, which would be permanent. The prisoner stated that he had been defending himself from the rough treatment of the police. The jury returned a verdict of 'guilty' and he was sentenced to a term of eighteen months' imprisonment.

6 AUGUST 1892 An inquest was held at Wigan before coroner Mr Rowbottom, touching the death of 44-year-old John Moran. Kate Glancey, wife

THE ALLEGED MANSLAUGHTER AT WIGAN.

The alleged manslaughter case at Wigan, 1892.

of a Scholes grocer, was charged with the death and attended the inquest. It was stated that Moran and Glancey had been arguing and the latter had ordered Moran out of the house, saying that if he did not go, she would 'brain' him. Moran left the house but Glancey followed him into the yard and hit him on the head with a kettle. The man died about an hour afterwards – death was caused by concussion of the brain brought about by his head wounds. Bridget Lavans stated that she saw a man named Gibbons throw the deceased upon the ground, so that his head came into contact with the flags, and denied that Mrs Glancey was present. Catherine Murphy corroborated this statement. Patrick Gibbons denied the allegations made against him. Michael Moran, the brother of the deceased, said that Glancey's husband had promised to pay for the funeral if the matter was kept quiet. The jury returned a verdict of 'manslaughter' against Glancey and she was committed for trial at the Assizes.

7 AUGUST 1888 John Jackson was in Strangeways Prison, serving six months for burglary. The prison authorities knew that Jackson was a skilled plumber and asked if he cared to renew some piping in a house occupied by the prison matron. Jackson agreed to do the work and was taken to the job by Ralph Webb, a prison officer whom Jackson knew well. It was early in the afternoon when the matron heard a muffled cry coming from the bedroom where Jackson and the prison officer were. On investigating, she found the room locked from the inside. Other officers were soon at the scene, and breaking down the door they found their colleague had been beaten to death with a hammer – a hole in the ceiling revealed where Jackson had made his escape. Despite a massive manhunt, it was several weeks before Jackson was recaptured, after breaking into a house in Bradford. He was tried for the murder of Webb, found guilty and hanged at Strangeways on 7 August 1888. James Berry, the hangman, was said to have given a sly grin as he pulled the bolt on the scaffold drop – after all, prison warden Ralph Webb used to be a firm friend of his.

1881 There was a terrible train crash at Blackburn railway station resulting in a number of fatalities. An express train left Manchester at 2.25 p.m. to arrive at Blackburn Station at 3 o'clock. It then should have proceeded to Hellifield to meet the Midland Express to Scotland. A train from Liverpool was standing in Blackburn Station. As the Manchester train came towards the station the brakes were applied, but for some unaccountable reason they failed. The train went dashing ahead and crashed into a shunting engine; the stationary Liverpool train and carriages all piled up in the collision. Would-be passengers on the station platform could only look on in horror at the carnage before them. Scores of people were injured in the crash, and first reports indicated that five people had been killed. These were: Mrs Alice Hargreaves from Over Darwen; Charles Lomas Tiplady, an accountant from Blackburn; Victoriani de Ysasi, a Spaniard wine merchant from London; Mrs Swift from Bradford; and a young lady aged just 14 from Southport, who died at the Infirmary the following Wednesday.

8 AUGUST

How the scene might have appeared after the train crash at Blackburn Station. (Taken from an old newspaper report)

The Tinker & Budget pub, where the inquest was held on Adam Cowell.

9 AUGUST **1862** Adam Cowell, a 37-year-old mason, was killed in an accident at Oswaldtwistle. Adam was working on a scaffold whilst erecting some new houses at New Lane, when the scaffold gave way and he was precipitated to the ground. He survived until the following Friday when he passed away. An inquest was held at the Tinker & Budget, where a verdict of 'accidental death' was returned.

10 AUGUST **1850** An inquest was held at the Bee Hive public house in Horwich on the body of Larael Whitehead, a 20-year-old labourer who died as a consequence of being stabbed in the breast with the prongs of a hay fork on 7 July. Whitehead, along with two men named Richard Barlow and John Snape, went to a pond on John Fletcher's farm, intending to take his fish. Mr Fletcher became alarmed on hearing his dogs bark; he went out and saw the three men, then armed himself with a hay fork – the handle of which was several feet long – and went to the pond to drive them away. Two of the men went up to Mr Fletcher while the other tried to draw the net, and a scuffle ensued in which Whitehead was stabbed in the chest with the fork. He was conveyed home, where he lingered until the 7th inst. The jury returned a verdict of 'justifiable homicide'.

11 AUGUST **1850** Reports on an atrocious child murder, which happened in Southport on 24 July, were being issued. A man walking over the sand hills near the Bold Arms had noticed a new-born child moving about half-buried in the sand-dunes. The child was taken to the house of Henry Mercer, who had it baptised the very same day. However, from the want of breast milk and exposure to the elements, the child wasted and died not long afterwards. An 'idiot woman' named Ann Ball was taken into custody over the offence. It seemed that she had delivered the child herself, and then placed it in her apron and carried it through the streets – it kicking and crying the whole time. She then dug a hole in the sand and buried the child whilst it was still alive. Neighbours,

seeing her on the dunes, thought she was killing a fowl. She was ordered to be transported for the term of her natural life.

1850   At around three o'clock in the afternoon, an explosion took place at the Lees & Mills Waterhead Mill, Oldham. This caused the death of boiler maker George Fox, and two other people were seriously scalded. The real cause of the accident is unknown, but it is supposed that the explosion arose from a defective pipe giving way in the flue tubes. In the building there were two boilers, one of which was undergoing a slight repair, and it was on this boiler that Mr Fox and his men were working. In consequence of this boiler being out of work, the looms, throstles and dressing frames had been stopped, so the explosion was apparently not caused by pressure. There was an 18in-long rent in a tube where the rivets had been torn out. When this took place, water rushed into the fire, the steam forcing the massive doors and framework to a distance of 12ft and blowing down all the brickwork in front of the boiler. At that moment, Mr Fox was passing in front to give some instruction to his men and took the whole force of the scalding steam. He was removed to a neighbouring cottage and help was procured, but he died at about two o'clock the following day.

12 AUGUST

1826   Robert Parkinson was charged with killing John Ward at Nova Scotia, near Blackburn, on 28 March by running over him with his coach. As Parkinson was driving in Blackburn, Ward, an old man who was blind in one eye and deaf, was crossing the road; he was knocked down by the fore horse of the coach. His shoulder was dislocated, his thigh broken, and he received injuries to the back – the man died in seven weeks. After hearing further evidence, the jury found the prisoner 'not guilty' and he was discharged.

13 AUGUST

1876   Emily Holland, aged just 7, boasted to all her young friends in Birley Street, Blackburn about her new 'uncle'; she had met him in the street and was now going to run some errands for him. Poor Emily was never seen alive again. After an extensive two-day search by the local constabulary, her torso was found in a field – minus her arms and head. She had been brutally raped and her body dismembered – some body parts were later found wrapped in newspaper. Robert Taylor, a tramp, was arrested two weeks later as the local children identified him as the person Emily had claimed to be her new 'uncle'. However, some of the other locals suspected a shopkeeper named William Fish, whose shop was in nearby Moss Street. The police turned their investigation towards Fish; in his shop they found copies of the *Preston Herald* with pages missing which corresponded exactly with those in which Emily's body parts had

14 AUGUST

WILLIAM FISH

FATAL FIRE AT BAILEY&Co'S MILLS BOLTON

Above left: William Fish, the murderer of Emily Holland.

Above right: The great mill fire at Bolton in 1882.

been wrapped. A bloodhound had been used to find the missing body parts, and, when the dog was taken to Fish's shop, it began barking frantically at the fireplace. When the police investigated the chimney they found bloody copies of the *Manchester Courier* and the rest of Emily's body. An angry lynch mob gathered outside of the shop, and Fish had to be smuggled out by the back door. The tramp was released, and Fish was found guilty of the horrendous offence. He was hanged for his crime at Kirkdale Prison on 14 August 1876.

15 AUGUST   1844   Thomas Redford, a hairdresser from Little Bolton, was brought before the borough court at Bolton to face the charge of shaving on the previous Sunday, in breach of the Sabbath. It was claimed that this case was an acceptance under the Act as it was a necessity that a man should be shaved and cleaned to enable him to go to the place of worship. The prosecution, however, contended that Sunday shaving was unnecessary as any person could get shaved the previous night. It was also contended that nine tenths of those who got shaved on Sunday were either half drunk, or had been drunk on Saturday night. After a short recess, the defendant was fined 5s and costs.

16 AUGUST   1882   There was a great fire at the mill belonging to Messrs Bailey & Co. at Bolton, which resulted in loss of life. The fire started at around three o'clock and soon the operatives making their escape found the building falling in around them amidst scenes of fearful confusion. The point of ignition was a pair of spinning mules near the stairway on the second floor. Several persons were injured running into the sharp ends

of the machinery, and some by jumping out of the windows to escape the flames – one woman perished in the blaze and the damage amounted to £60,000.

1827   In the small hamlet of Claughton, lying to the east of Garstang, Betty Plimley heard a violent quarrel between her neighbours William Robinson, aged 34, and his wife Ellen. The matter appeared to have been resolved, and the following day Betty went to her neighbours' house to make dinner for Ellen, who was not in the best of health. William was out of the house at that time, and just before twelve o'clock Ellen also left the house. When William came home soon afterwards, he asked where his wife was – but Betty could not say. William stormed out, but returned within a short time saying he could not find her. Ellen apparently went to and from her house all that afternoon, but each time missed her husband. Eventually, around 4.30 p.m., the pair met up inside the house and William asked her if she thought such 'carryings on' would do. She made no reply, but simply went upstairs. Ellen then shouted something to her husband, who rushed upstairs. Betty – all the time observing the proceedings – then heard several blows being struck upstairs and Ellen shouted out, 'William, thou hast done enough!' William shouted back loudly, 'No, I have not!' This was followed by the sound of several more blows; William Robinson had murdered his wife. He was charged with the offence and taken to Lancaster to stand trial. There he was found guilty and was sentenced to death by hanging; it was also ordered that his body be dissected. William stood in the dock, and up until then had flattered himself that he would get away with the lesser charge of manslaughter. When the sentence was passed he gasped and stared wildly about the courtroom. He had to be removed from the bar in a state of near collapse.

1908   Twenty-seven lives were lost at the Maypole Colliery in the Wigan Coalfield of Lancashire on 18 August 1908. Fund-raising for the victims of the disaster took several forms, one of which was the distribution of postcards with the following verse:

Don't go down the mine daddy
A miner was leaving his home for work
When he heard his little child scream
He went to his bedside, his little white face,
'Oh daddy, I've had such a dream,
I dreamt that I saw the pit all afire
And men struggled hard for their lives
The scene it then changed, and the top of the mine
Was surrounded by sweethearts and wives.

Don't go down the mine dad,
Dreams very often come true,
Daddy you know it would break my heart
If anything happened to you.
Just go and tell my dream to your mates
And as true as the stars that shine
Something is going to happen today
Dear daddy don't go down the mine.

The miner, a man with heart good and kind
Sat by the side of his son
He said 'It's my living, I can't stay away,
For duty my lad must be done'.
The little lad looked up, and sadly he said
'Oh please stay today with me dad'
But as the brave miner went forth to his work,
He heard this appeal from his lad

Whilst waiting his turn with his mates to descend
He could not banish his fears
He returned home again to his wife and his child
Those words seemed to ring through to his ears.
And when the day ended, the pit was on fire
When a score of brave men lost their lives
He thanked God above for the dream his child had,
As once more the little one cried.

19 AUGUST 1872 An inquest was held at the Hob Inn, Bamber Bridge touching on the death of a 10-year-old boy named Thomas Alstead who was killed at Mr Dewhurst's Mill at Cuerden. The deceased boy was a creeler working under his father, and whilst cleaning some machinery he was caught in it and died a few minutes afterwards. The jury returned a verdict of 'accidental death'.

20 AUGUST 1899 A shocking murder occurred at Whitworth, a few miles from Rochdale. A quarryman named Michael Dowdle, an old soldier who had seen active service in South Africa, had for some time had an unhappy relationship with his wife in consequence of him giving way to drink. The wife by all accounts was hard-working and respectable, and had left him the previous week. However, her husband had enticed her back to the family home. After sending the five children out to play, an argument ensued and Dowdle slit her throat with a knife, before giving himself up

Michael Dowdle, caught in the act of murdering his wife.

to the police. He was found guilty of the murder and, on Wednesday, 6 December 1899, was hanged for the crime at Manchester.

1852 Victorian newspapers left nothing to the imagination when it came to reporting fatal accidents, and gave little thought for those left behind to grieve – take this report from the *Manchester Guardian* of Wednesday, 25 August 1852:

21 AUGUST

> One of the most deplorable accidents that have occurred in this neighbourhood for some time took place at Leyland Mill Foundry Wigan on Saturday forenoon last. It appears that John Kearsley, the driver of the steam engine at the works was in the habit of tightening some of the straps of the machinery while the engine was still at work. He seems to have been thus employed when he was caught by the arm and carried up to the shaft, at that time supposed to be running at four or five hundred revolutions per minute. His arm was twisted round until it was torn off from his shoulder, when he fell amongst the machinery below, where his throat was cut and his head severed from his body. His arm was found with a leather thong or lace, together with his shirt sleeve, twisted tight around it, and his shirt had been ripped from the waist upwards. The unfortunate man was 38 years of age, and has left a wife and two children.

22 AUGUST **1849** John Gleeson Wilson appeared before Liverpool Assizes charged with the murder of Mary Parr, a housemaid living at 20 Leveson Street, Liverpool. The evidence showed that Wilson had enquired about lodging at the house of Ann Hinrichson in Leveson Street and was taken in, even though he had not one penny to his name. He settled in and, on the second day, Mrs Hinrichson went shopping, leaving Wilson with her two sons and the maid, Mary Parr. What followed was a horrific attack on the residents; he knocked the maid unconscious, beat the older child Harold to death with a shovel, then slit the throat of the young child Alfred. The motive was obviously robbery, for when Mrs Hinrichson came home soon afterwards, Wilson was rifling through some of her belongings. She screamed, and as she turned to run she saw her dead children before her. Wilson caught her and beat her half to death with a poker, then left the house – a delivery boy raised the alarm as he noticed the chaos through the open doorway. Both children were dead, but Mrs Hinrichson and the maid were still alive – although both later died from their injuries. John Gleeson Wilson was found guilty of Mary Parr's murder and was sentenced to death. He was hanged at Kirkdale Prison on 15 September before a crowd of almost 100,000 spectators. Leveson Street was renamed Grenville Street, but, for many years, sightseers still pointed out No. 20, where the bloodbath had taken place. All of the victims were buried in St James's Cemetery, Liverpool.

23 AUGUST **1944** Two American Liberator bomber aircraft left Warton Airfield at 10.30 a.m. on a test flight. One was soon in serious trouble as it hit a storm being swept in from the Irish Sea. The pilot turned the aeroplane back inland through the now atrocious weather, struggling to keep control. By the time it was approaching Freckleton, it was flying very low – the wings of the aircraft were near vertical. The plane then ripped the top off a tree, and shed its right wingtip as it chopped off the corner of a building, leaving the rest of the wing ploughing along the ground through a field hedge. The bomber, weighing in at 25 tons, carried on. It then partly demolished three houses and the Sad Sack Snack Bar. The plane's momentum spurred it onwards, taking it across Lytham Road at Freckleton. Finally the plane came to rest in a ball of flames as it destroyed the infants' wing of Freckleton Holy Trinity School. The clock in one of the school classrooms stopped at 10.47 a.m. The horror of that day showed that sixty-one lives were lost in total, as some who were not killed outright later succumbed to their injuries. Thirty-eight children perished, along with two teachers, and twenty-one civilians and service personnel. One of the teachers, Miss Jenny Hall, had only started work at the school the day before; most of the children were aged just 4, 5 and 6 years old. Around Freckleton

"This is the site of the village school where, on the 23rd August 1944, during a severe storm, an American bomber crashed with the loss of 61 lives."

This included 38 children, 2 teachers and 21 civilians and service personnel.

Always in Our Hearts

This plaque on Trinity Close recalls the terrible air disaster which claimed sixty-one lives, and is erected near the site of the ill-fated village school. (Jack Nadin)

there are a number of memorials to this sad accident, including a communal grave in Holy Trinity churchyard with the names of those who died. On the first anniversary of the disaster, a Memorial Garden and children's play area, constructed by American servicemen, was opened. The site of the former village school is now modern housing, on what is now named Trinity Close.

1904 Susan Westwell, a 78-year-old widowed woman of Hyndburn Road, Accrington, was always considered by the locals as rather peculiar. She used to lend pennies to the mill workers or anyone else who was interested, and to supplement her income would also brew tea for the factory operatives. On Wednesday, 24 August 1904, the old widow was found bludgeoned to death by intruders at her home; the house had been systematically ransacked and she was found lying behind her front door. A neighbour who called at her house shortly before noticed two unidentified youths sitting on the wall outside her house, but they were never traced. As the local folks put it later, 'It will forever more remain a mystery, unless someone blabs.' **24 AUGUST**

1845 It was around dinnertime when Robert Brown, a coal proprietor, was discovered in his pigeon loft, near his Westhoughton residence, suspended from the roof by a rope. He was quickly cut down, but all signs of life had ceased. The unfortunate gentleman had lately been engaged in some mining operations at Chequerbent, in which it was thought that he had lost a great deal of money. This, and a depression of his mind, probably led to his rash act – he left a family and was aged around 50 years old. **25 AUGUST**

26 AUGUST **1879** Martha Rothwell, a 21-year-old servant girl in the employ of Miss Halstead of Hood House, Manchester Road, Burnley, was accidentally shot dead by William Baker, a butler at the same household. Baker had

FATAL GUN ACCIDENT at BURNLEY

The accidental shooting of Martha Rothwell in 1879.

been out shooting rats and went into the pantry, which overlooked the back yard of the house, to clean his gun. Two servants were then at the window, and Baker said 'Look out Martha', and accidentally touched the trigger. The shot passed through her head ear-to-ear, killing her instantly. He was later brought before the courts on a charge of killing her, but was liberated – the Bench having strong words on the way he went about cleaning his weapon.

27 AUGUST **1866** A boiler exploded on board the steam ship *Talbot*, near the mouth of Morecambe Bay. Those on board were startled by the noise and rushed to the decks to find the engine room filled with steam. Later it was found that the chief engineer Robert Livingstone, the second engineer Robert Lamb, and a fireman had been seriously scalded. Livingstone and the fireman died the following day from their injuries.

28 AUGUST **1948** Margaret Allen was born to a large family in Rawtenstall, but she was a lonely, unhappy girl for most of her life. As she approached maturity she gained a strong masculine personality, and even began to dress like a man. She had her hair cut short, wore a trilby hat, and preferred to be known as 'Bill'. In 1942 she got a job as a bus conductor with Rawtenstall Corporation – a job she enjoyed at last – until her mother died a year later. This had a drastic effect on 'Bill', who became depressed and ill-kempt whilst living in her run-down stone cottage at 137 Bacup Road. She soon afterwards became acquainted with an elderly lady, Nancy Ellen Chadwick, known in the district as a fortune teller and miser. Nancy Ellen would often sit in the parks of Rawtenstall counting her money, and it was probably here that 'Bill' Allen met her. Early in the morning of 29 August 1948, Nancy Ellen Chadwick was spotted lying dead in the road almost outside 'Bill' Allen's cottage. She had severe head injuries from a rain of blows inflicted with a blunt instrument. When Margaret Allen's cottage was searched, there was blood all over the walls and back door, and she confessed to the crime. She had intended, she said, to dispose of the body in the river Irwell, but finding it too heavy simply abandoned it in the street. A plea of insanity at Manchester Assizes in December failed to impress anyone, and she was sentenced to death. A petition for her reprieve failed to gather any strength and was only signed by 152 of the 26,000-strong population of Rawtenstall. She was hanged at Strangeways Prison on 12 January 1949. On the gallows she was said to have uttered, 'It might help if I could cry, but my manhood holds back any tears.'

29 AUGUST **1892** At 7.30 a.m., James Rothwell, a stoker employed at the West Leigh Coal Company's pit at Leigh, South Lancashire, was standing in front of the engine boiler when it exploded. Rothwell was blown a distance of 18ft across the yard, against a wall, where he was found dead. His whole body was terribly scalded.

30 AUGUST **1869** The murder of 32-year-old Ann Shandley was reported on. Ann's husband, Walter Shandley, killed her in the Cheshire Cheese pub on Oldham Road, Manchester on 22 August. After the killing, Walter immediately made his escape. The whole incident began when Walter asked his wife to leave the public house; she had refused, being rather worse for wear, saying that it was not time to go yet. Shandley hit her, although by all accounts it was not a hard or serious blow. She was, however, dead by the time she was seen by Mr Bentflower, the junior surgeon at the Royal Infirmary. Walter Shandley gave himself up a short time later to PC Gibson in Blossom Street,

The killing of Ann Shandley by her husband Walter in the Cheshire Cheese public house in 1869.

Great Ancoats, where he confessed to the killing. Following the inquest he was put on a charge of manslaughter, although it is not known whether he was found guilty or not guilty.

31 AUGUST **1869** There were three suicides in Preston Jail this month. Daniel Carmichael, a Scottish seaman aged 18, had been convicted seven times for various crimes in Scotland, and at the last Preston Sessions he was sentenced to two years for housebreaking. He always complained about the food given to him in prison. One Monday he refused to eat his meal, and when he asked for it back he was told he could not have it. That afternoon he threw a stone at the deputy governor and rushed at him with a knife. The following Wednesday he was found in his cell hanging from a gas pipe. The jury returned a verdict of 'hanged himself; state of mind not known'.

SEPTEMBER

Turton Tower, where the Timberbottom Skulls rest in peace – but the apparition of the Black Lady still wanders through the ancient hall, or so it is said. (*See* 8 September.) (Jack Nadin)

1 SEPTEMBER **1848** William Oliver, one of the county policemen, was brought up before the Rochdale Petty Sessions on a charge of being drunk and disorderly. At about ten o'clock on the previous Tuesday evening, at a beerhouse in Baillie Street, he had removed some of his clothes and was very unruly. He should have been on duty at that time, and it was stated that he had been fined before for a similar offence. Oliver pleaded that he had met a friend whom he had not seen for twenty-one years, and they had been having a drink together. The case was ordered to be decided by Captain Woodford, chief constable of the county.

2 SEPTEMBER **1855** There was a terrible boiler explosion at the mill belonging to Lancaster & Isherwood on Ribbleton Lane, Preston, by which William Crombleholme was killed. At the inquest, it was considered that the explosion was due to the neglect of the engine tenter, who was subsequently committed on a charge of manslaughter.

3 SEPTEMBER **1883** Several Irish navvies assembled at the Baker's Arms, a beerhouse in Lawson Street, Preston. Unable to work because of the bad weather, they had little choice but to spend the day in the pub. Amongst the men were Patrick M'Ginty, aged about 32, and Anthony Henry, his cousin, who was about the same age. To pass the time the men started playing cards, and within a short time Henry accused M'Ginty of unfair play and an argument ensued. However, others calmed the situation down and the men seemed to make up. Both men later went to stand outside, along with a number of others. Anthony Henry then left the crowd and went off towards his lodgings, returning a few minutes later with his brother Patrick. M'Ginty and the others were still standing at the doorway of the inn when, without warning, Henry pulled from his trousers 'something like a cleaver' and struck M'Ginty a savage blow on the temple. Blood gushed from the wound and M'Ginty dropped to the floor. The injured man was

Murderer Anthony Henry takes his opportunity to escape during the commotion that followed his attack at Preston.

taken to the Infirmary but died at seven o'clock without recovering consciousness. Henry disappeared in the commotion, and at the inquest was charged with the murder of his cousin in his absence. A reward of £100 was offered for his arrest, but as far as I am aware Anthony Henry was never brought to justice.

1844 Kirkham Bennett, owner of the 'Neptune' four-horse coach 4 SEPTEMBER
on the daily run from Bolton, employed a man named Tiplady as driver. When the coach pulled into the White Horse Inn at Leigh, a stable hand noticed that the shoulders of two of the horses were completely raw for the breadth of a man's hand. One of the horses sat down upon its haunches and would not stir; two others would not draw as they were so sore. The fourth was willing to draw the coach, but it was on this horse that the coachman wreaked his anger, by beating him in a fearful manner. The poor beasts had to be led out on to the road, in some cases with two or more drivers beating them. The case was reported to the authorities and taken to court.

The White Horse, where the coach horses were cruelly treated in 1844, was demolished in 1898 for the widening of Market Street.

Here it was stated that the proprietor of this coach had attained notoriety throughout the land for the bad treatment his horses received. Bennett appeared for his servant, but the magistrate told him that the blame did not fall upon his servant, but upon himself. The case was dismissed in this instance with a condition of paying the expenses, and a warning that if such a case was brought before the magistrates again they would deal with it most severely.

1890 Four-year-old Martin Gibbons had a remarkable escape when he 5 SEPTEMBER
fell out of the Southport Express as it was pulling out of Aintree Station. The train was travelling quite fast at the time and Mrs Gibbons – and several of the passengers – tried pulling the cord to stop it, but unfortunately the cord got tangled up with the open door and broke. Martin was picked

A narrow escape from death on the Southport Express.

up by a woman near Black Bull Bridge – he was injured and had to be taken to Stanley Hospital in Liverpool, although he had escaped being killed.

6 SEPTEMBER   **1841**   It was Oldham Wakes, and according to custom a number of men were drawing a 'rush cart' along Mumps, near Oldham. Edward Whittaker, in a state of intoxication, tried to get amongst the people who were pulling the cart. A scuffle ensued, and the men pulling the cart set off at a pace to overtake another cart just in front of them. Whittaker got thrown down and the wheel of the cart ran over his leg. He was quickly taken up and conveyed to the Friendship public house, then to the Oldham Poor house, and finally to the Manchester Infirmary where he died four days later. The inquest heard evidence that a main artery in his leg had been severed, causing extensive bleeding, and returned a verdict of 'accidental death'.

7 SEPTEMBER   **1876**   An inquest was held at Fleetwood on the body of George Stevens, a Private who was found on a bench at Fleetwood with two bullet holes in him. Stevens, along with a party of other men, had gone from Fulwood Barracks to Fleetwood for ball practice. At about 10.30 on the previous Monday, the deceased and another man were in the Queen's Hotel and decided to have a shooting match. The following day, Stevens' body was found with a gun lying beside it, and another gun was discovered 40 yards away in the water. Enquiries revealed that the other man was named Kelly; he was later arrested and charged with murder, even though he maintained that the gun had gone off accidentally. The case was later thrown out by the courts, there being no evidence to support the charge.

8 SEPTEMBER   **1931**   Lady Nina Knowles bequeathed the Turton Tower to Turton Urban District Council to benefit the local community after the death of her husband, Sir Lees Knowles. Turton Tower is roughly 3 miles north of Bolton, and was built as a simple defensive structure by the Turbocs, Lord of the Manor, around 1200. It was strengthened by the Orrell family, who came into possession through marriage, and the east and north-east wings were added in the sixteenth century. Turton Tower is perhaps best known for the 'Timberbottom Skulls', on display here on a Bible in a glass case. The skulls, of a man and woman, were found in Bradshaw Brook around 1750 and taken to a local farm, now demolished, named Timberbottom. From then on, any attempt to move, or remove, the skulls gave rise to a variety of supernatural events – unaccountable knocking and banging, blood-curdling screams, and furniture moving of its own accord.

In 1840, the Timberbottom tenants had the skulls buried in Bradshaw churchyard, but the supernatural activities became so intense that the skulls had to be exhumed and returned to Timberbottom. When the farm was demolished the skulls were moved to Bradshaw Hall, until it too was demolished in the 1950s, and the skulls were then presented to Turton Tower – along with other valuable antiques – by Colonel Hardcastle. Here they remain in silent contentment, but only as long as they are not removed from the glass case or the Bible. Turton Tower, like any other self-respecting old hall, has its own ghost – a lady in black. She has often been seen ascending a spiral staircase to the top floor of the house.

1826   Mr Mawdsley, a respectable liquor merchant from Ormskirk, was on a shooting excursion accompanied by friends. During the course of the day, Mr Mawdsley (who had taken with him a flask of spirit) retired to a water pit for the purpose of mixing water with his liquor. He did not return for a considerable time, and, when his friends went to seek him out, they discovered that he had fallen head-first into the pit and drowned. All attempts to restore animation failed.

9 SEPTEMBER

1846   An inquest was held at Preston on the body of Margaret Bromley of Edward Street West. A druggist, whose shop was on Marsh Lane, stated that Margaret had visited his shop on the previous Saturday to buy some arsenic to mix with whitewash for the purpose of killing bugs. He told her that he did not sell it by itself, and that she would have to bring along the whitewash and he would then mix it in for her. She returned with an earthenware jug containing about four quarts of whitewash and purchased 2*d* worth of arsenic, which the druggist added to the wash. James Bromley, Margaret's husband, said that he had been at home on Saturday night, but on the request of his wife he went out. He returned at ten o'clock and found his wife vomiting. One of the children said that she had taken arsenic, but she insisted that she had not. Margaret persisted in saying that she had not taken any poison – until Sunday morning, when at last she confessed to having taken 2*d* worth of arsenic mixed with whitewash. Her husband sent for the surgeon, Mr Booth, who

10 SEPTEMBER

The druggist's shop where Margaret Bromley purchased poison.

attended her until her death the following Thursday at 2 a.m. She had taken poison on other occasions, and had recently been in very low spirits. The jury returned a verdict of 'lunacy'.

11 SEPTEMBER 1875 John Henry Howarth was summoned for assault at Burnley. On 21 August, his wife Martha was leaving the market when her husband struck her in the face. As she got to the Cross Keys, he struck her again. She said she would summons him and he retorted that he would cut her head off. She had not gone much further when he dragged her to the ground by her hair and kicked her leg several times, making it black. He also tore her dress and broke her umbrella. She screamed out, and her husband ran off. It was implied that the woman was leading an immoral life, and her husband had seen her that day with another woman and a man named Dewhurst. The Bench inflicted a penalty of 20s and costs, or one month's imprisonment.

The Cross Keys Hotel at Burnley, where Martha Howarth was brutally beaten by her husband in 1875.

12 SEPTEMBER 1849 Several owners and occupiers of dwelling houses and cellars in Cook Street, Posey Row, Posey Street, Premium Street and Lowe Street were summoned by Salford Borough Court under the Nuisances Removal and Diseases Prevention Act for having their houses in a filthy state, and the ashpits and privies in an objectionable condition. It was stated by the Town Clerk that six or eight fatal cases of cholera had occurred in Cook Street, and four in Lowe Street. Most of the owners charged agreed to have the nuisances removed, and an order was granted in each case. Robert Jackson, agent for some of the houses in Posey Row, complained that the majority of the houses there had been unoccupied for several years because of the smells coming from the gas works, and he thought that the gas committee should also be prosecuted. A man named William Hibbert, the tenant of a yard in Rosamond Street, was summoned for keeping thirty to forty pigs in the yard. In his defence it was stated that his was the best piggery in town

in point of cleanliness. Robert Slinger, a butcher, was summoned for a nuisance arising from a slaughterhouse and some pigsties in Park Street – for which an order was made for removal.

1864 The *Manchester Guardian* reported:

Yesterday morning, William Berry, miller living at 20 Ormskirk Road, Preston murdered his wife, and afterwards attempted to commit suicide. Since Whitsuntide the man has been in a depressed state, particularly through business affairs, and to some extent through certain family affairs. He seems to have been jealous of his wife, although it is said for no reason whatever. On Monday Berry and his wife took lodgings on Ormskirk Road, and their children, two in number, were removed to some of their relatives. Early yesterday morning Berry's wife was heard screaming, and it was subsequently discovered that she had been stabbed several times about her breast, and that her throat had been cut. Her windpipe was cut completely through – she bled very profusely and died about half an hour after she had been found. Berry was found sitting on the bed with his throat cut, and the latest reports are that he is unlikely to survive.

The following evidence has been prepared and forwarded to the magistrates for a hearing today. Edward Leach, of 29 Ormskirk Road says: 'About half past five o'clock I heard a scream in the room where the deceased and her husband were sleeping. I went to their room and saw the deceased at the window. Her husband was at the side of the bed and I seized him. Directly I took hold of him, he made a stab at his own throat with a pocket knife. He made several stabs at his throat. He said 'Let me do it quietly Ned'. Another witness stated that before she died the deceased told him that her husband had cut her throat. Inspector Hornby states, that when he asked Berry why he had committed the crime, the man replied 'It was through some men being in the house last night.' Yesterday morning Berry was visited by a priest. He expressed some sorrow at what he had done, and said that he knew that he had committed murder.

1827 The *Manchester Guardian* reported:

This morning at eight o' clock, William Robinson, who was on Friday convicted of the wilful murder of his wife, Ellen Robinson at Claughton near Garstang paid the forfeit of his life in expiation of his crime. The unhappy man appeared extremely resigned to his fate – but to the last solemnly declared his innocence of any intension [*sic*] to kill his wife, and denied that he had done anything to strangle, or strike her otherwise than with his fists. After hanging the usual time the body was cut down, and, in pursuance of the sentence, delivered to the surgeons for dissection.

15 SEPTEMBER

1838 Inglewhite is a pretty little village to the north of Preston with its own ancient market cross and a scattering of charming cottages around the village green. But, in 1838, the tiny community was thrust into the national headlines. Ann Sanderson was married to Edward Sanderson, a humble, honest and hard-working labourer, and they lived in a cottage on Fairhurst Lane. The couple were happily married and had five young children. Ann, however, always considered herself to be above the working class, and received a regular sum from her mother which elevated her quality of life slightly. This was all very well until her mother suddenly died, and the regular contribution to Ann's higher standard of living ceased. Ann bitterly resented this, and tried to borrow money to maintain her previous lifestyle – but to no avail. Her position in the little rural community, where she had previously been looked upon with high esteem, now looked grim; whispered comments spread around the village, suggesting that Ann Sanderson was not as well off as she made out. Ann turned into a tormented woman; she sought solace in the church and became deeply religious. Around July 1838, she bought some arsenic from Garstang and, on 15 September, she slowly poured the arsenic into a flour pudding, which she and her five children ate for

St Mary's Church, Goosnargh – the final resting place of Ann Sanderson and her five children. (Jack Nadin)

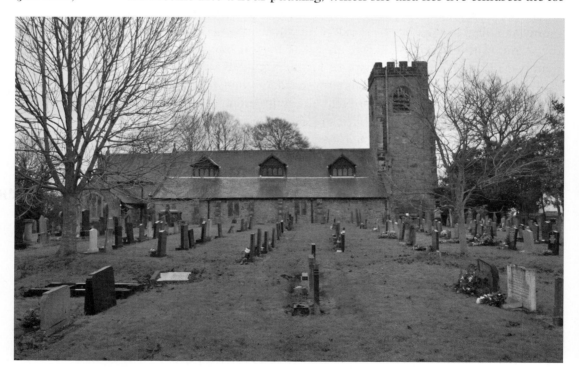

dinner – the result being the death of all six individuals. It was a scene to break the hardest of hearts as the woman and her five little innocents were lowered into the same grave at Goosnargh churchyard. During the ceremony, not an inch of ground near the grave which commanded a view was vacant, and tears ran freely.

1864 The *Manchester Guardian* reported: 16 SEPTEMBER

> Last night James Heaton, landlord of the 'Coach and Horses Inn', Church Lane Oldham, died from the effects of scalding. He rose at an early hour in the morning to brew and whilst emptying a quantity of malt into the mash tub, he fell in, the liquid then being almost at boiling point. The poor man succeeded in getting out of the vessel, and managed to crawl into the lobby of the house, where his groans awoke the inmates. He was found to be dreadfully burnt, the skin peeling off his back when the removal of his clothes was attempted. Every assistance was rendered, but he died after lingering about 16 hours in great agony.

1872 It was almost 5.30 p.m. and a great thunderstorm and gale   17 SEPTEMBER
raged over Littleborough. The 'electric fluid' struck the five-storey high Frankfort Mills, which had burnt down only three weeks previous. The walls of the mill fell inwards, and the steel and falling masonry buried six people who were inside cleaning up after the fire. Mr Heap, the mill manager, called for help and a number of mill operatives were soon on the scene. Within ten minutes the first of the victims was rescued; his name was Charles Rigg, a resident of Featherstall. His legs were badly crushed and he had bruising about the head. The next to be relieved was 14-year-old Ellen Sagar, she was cut about the head but nothing too serious. The rest of the victims were all unfortunately killed. These included 13-year-old Elizabeth Ann Mason, 18-year-old Elizabeth Jane Harrison, 19-year-old Mary Davine, and 27-year-old Sarah Stott.

1786 James Holland, a lad in his late teens, came from a poor Bolton   18 SEPTEMBER
family. Near his home were the tenter fields, where cloth was hung out after being bleached to dry on tenter hooks. James, his belly rumbling with hunger, wondered whether the sale of just one or two pieces of cloth would be enough to ease the pangs of his empty belly. He knew that stealing cloth was a hanging offence, but temptation and hunger proved too much. He stole several yards of cloth belonging to Mr Thwaite – unfortunately for him he was seen. Justice was quick in those days, and he was tried, found guilty and sentenced to a public execution on Bolton Moor. A large crowd assembled and the employers of the

neighbourhood dragged their workmen to the scene as a deterrent, in case they thought about theft from the tenter fields. James's body dropped on the gallows and swung into eternity, his limp, lifeless body was then left suspended on Gallows Hill on Deane Moor as a further reminder of the penalties of crime.

19 SEPTEMBER   1832   The *Preston Chronicle* reported:

> An inquest was held before James Dixon, Mayor, one of the Coroners for this Borough [Preston], touching the death of an elderly man named Robert Worden, who had at an earlier hour on the same morning put a period to his existence by cutting his throat in a shocking manner with a razor. Michael Worden, the son of the deceased, stated his father had for a week past been in a very low and unsettled state of mind, owing to his having received a month's notice to quit his employment in the employ of Mr Tomlinson, the tanner, for whom he had worked for some time. On the afternoon of Tuesday, the deceased came home intoxicated and bewildered, and soon after went to bed. At seven in the evening he took some supper, and it was supposed he had gone to sleep. About four o'clock the following morning, a witness while still in bed, hearing a strange noise, went downstairs, without dressing, and on going into the front shop, stepped into some blood. He ran for assistance and gave the alarm. Mr Monk, surgeon, and some neighbours came in, and a light being procured, they found the deceased on the floor with his throat cut – and a razor near him – with which he had no doubt committed self-destruction. He was instantly lifted up, but life was found to be extinct. The jury after hearing the evidence returned a verdict to the effect that the deceased had destroyed himself during a fit of insanity.

20 SEPTEMBER   1857   At about 12 o'clock, Constable James Brierley was approached by a youth named Ashworth in Drake Street (Rochdale), who requested that the officer go into the Baptist Chapel to see if his brother was there, as he was afraid to go in himself. The youth said that his brother, 37-year-old Henry Ashworth, was the chapel keeper, and that he had left home at about six o'clock and had not been seen since. The officer entered the chapel, finding the door open, and noticed that it was dark inside. On the left-hand side there was a clock hanging about 4 yards from the floor. Beneath it the officer found a ladder, which appeared to have fallen, and Ashworth was lying on one side nearby, quite dead. There were no external marks of injury, except about the mouth. It was supposed that while winding the clock up, Henry Ashworth had fallen down. He had been unwell for several years.

1844   The *Manchester Guardian* reported on a strange phenomenon whereby some men who were boring a hole in the ground for Bickershaw Collieries heard a strange noise, and felt a rush of air from within the borehole. Cautiously they applied a light and, with the release of methane gas, a brilliant blue and orange flame 2-3 yards high was ignited. The gas continued to erupt for over a fortnight, before diminishing to half the original height and finally extinguishing itself altogether. The boring rods had reached the remarkable depth of 160 yards when the gas burst forth.

21 SEPTEMBER

1844   A new Improvement Act forbade customers from being in any alehouse, inn or tavern for the purpose of drinking after midnight. On 22 September 1844, a police watchman named Healey heard conversation from within the Bricklayer's Arms on Cheetham Street, Rochdale. Immediately on entering, the landlord, William Rigg, locked the door and took away the keys, saying to the watchman that he had no right to be in his house, and that he would make a prisoner of him. It was some time before the constable was released, and Rigg was later taken before the Rochdale Petty Sessions, where he was fined 10*s* and costs for the nocturnal imprisonment of the constable.

22 SEPTEMBER

1861   An inquest was held at the Royal Oak Inn at Garstang upon the body of Thomas Wilkinson Atkinson of Broughton-in-Cartmel, a surgeon aged 49 years. It appeared that about seven weeks previous, the deceased and his wife had taken lodgings with Mr Robert Noble, and from that time took to excessive drinking. On the Friday before his death, Atkinson was drinking ale, whisky and gin. Between the time he got up (at around 6.30 the next morning) and 4 p.m., he had a gill of gin and five pints of ale. About seven o'clock that evening, Dr Chapman was called in and found Atkinson somewhat excited, his breathing at times suspended, and loss of motion and sensibility over his entire body. He remained in that state until his death an hour later. Dr Chapman told the inquest that he thought the cause of death was either serum or blood upon the brain, caused by excessive drinking, and the jury returned a verdict to that effect.

23 SEPTEMBER

1872   Two men were working in the basement storeroom belonging to Jackson & Co. foundry on Hampson Street, Salford. Suddenly, the candle the men were carrying ignited fumes; one of the men rushed upstairs for some water, but the fire spread so rapidly that his companion was unable to make it out of the basement. The Salford Fire Service was soon on the spot, and when they extinguished the fire they found the poor man below a window as if trying to make his escape – but he had suffocated with the

24 SEPTEMBER

fumes and smoke. His name was William Brown, aged 40, who lived at Muslinet Street, Salford.

25 SEPTEMBER **1916** Helmshore is known today as the little weaving village near Haslingden where the 'textile museum' is. But, during the second year of the First World War, the villagers were alarmed to see a 500ft-long German Zeppelin droning overhead. It was making its way back from the Haslingden area where there was a gun cotton factory; as it reached Clod Lane, near Townsend Fold, Rawtenstall it let drop a bomb, causing some damage. After passing over Helmshore village, the Zeppelin slowly continued towards Holcombe, near Ramsbottom, where it inflicted more damage. The incident was a talking point for many years after the war.

26 SEPTEMBER **1857** The *Liverpool Mercury* reported:

> James Stewart one of the seamen on board the *Elizabeth Anne Bright*, from Liverpool, died from the cruelties received on board the vessel on her outward passage to Quebec. The Coroner's jury returned a verdict of 'Manslaughter' against Michael Keenan, the boatswain and declared that John Oliver, the commander of the *Elizabeth Anne Bright* is highly censurable for neglecting to provide the deceased James Stewart with the necessary care during his illness, and in not sending him to the hospital immediately on arriving in the port of Quebec.

27 SEPTEMBER **1857** An inquest was held by Mr Herford, city coroner, on the body of Catherine Hodkinson, aged 34, the wife of a tailor living in Salford. She had arrived at Ordsall Lane Station on Saturday night, by the train which left Liverpool at 6.30 p.m., and – against the advice of her fellow passengers – jumped out of the carriage before it came to a standstill. She consequently fell between the platform and the footboard, and the ticket collector heard her bones break as the wheels passed over her. Her right leg had been taken off, the left was broken, and she was otherwise seriously injured. She was taken to the Royal Infirmary where she died soon after nine o'clock. The jury returned a verdict of 'accidental death'.

28 SEPTEMBER **1889** The body of a man named George Gordon was discovered in a wardrobe in a furniture shop on Bolton Street, Bury, belonging to the Gordon Furniture Co. Mr Gordon, who was 30 years of age, had visited the shop on the previous day, and his father went looking for him when he did not return. The police became involved, but it was the father who noticed the wardrobe in the back room that contained the body. He asked William Dukes, a shop employee, to open the wardrobe

The scene inside the furniture shop when the murdered body of George Gordon was discovered inside a wardrobe.

up – but Dukes said he did not have the key. It was then broken into, and the body of George Gordon was revealed. He was a horrible sight; the head was battered in, there were several wounds about the face, the throat was cut and one of the eyes gouged out. Subsequently, Dukes was arrested for the murder. His trial, however, was postponed because after his arrest he became a witness in the case of a warder killing a prisoner at Strangeways. Finally he was tried in December 1889, and was found guilty and sentenced to death, being hanged on Christmas Eve 1889.

29 SEPTEMBER

1845 Ellen Platt, aged around 20, started out from the Bag Lane (Chowbent) Station with the intention of catching the 7.30 train to Liverpool. When she got to the Kenyon Junction it was necessary to change trains. She got out of the carriage on the wrong side and had to walk to the end of the train in order to reach the place where the Manchester train stopped. At that very moment a whistle was heard, and a train was seen rapidly approaching the track on which the unfortunate woman was on. A workman, witnessing what was happening, rushed forward to try and save her, but the buffer of the engine threw them both a considerable distance. They were both taken to the railway station and assistance was given by Mr Bradshaw of the Bolton line. An express engine was also sent off to Leigh, and, within the hour, Mr Brideoake, a surgeon, was on the spot – but it was too late for Ellen: she expired half an hour later. The man was expected to survive, and was conveyed to his house at Bolton.

30 SEPTEMBER **1862**   A large group of Irish harvesters were drinking at the Swan Inn in Kirkham – it was pay day and the ale was flowing. At eleven o'clock, the landlord, Henry Rawcliffe, asked them to drink up as it was closing time. One of their number refused to leave and so a constable was sent for, who took the man to the cells on account of his violent behaviour. This angered the rest of the gang, who gathered outside the Swan and began to shout and issue threats against the landlord. He was standing by a window when he was suddenly struck in the eye with an iron poker, which had been thrown from the crowd. It came with such force that it buried itself deep into his brain to a depth of 4in. The unfortunate Mr Rawcliffe fell immediately, and within the hour was a corpse. It took four men to pull the instrument of death from his brain. Two main suspects were brought before the Bench; they were Patrick Cain and Michael Kilburn. Cain actually confessed that he had thrown the poker, but not with any intent. He added, 'If they shall only spare my life I shall be content.' He was charged with manslaughter and later found guilty of the offence. Kilburn was released without charge.

OCTOBER

The terrible scene at Westhoughton when Henry Whittle murdered
his daughter-in-law and then committed suicide. (*See* 26 October.)

1 OCTOBER   **1875**   Ellen Ravenscroft, 11 years of age, was employed part time at the cotton mill of Mr Priestley in Euxton. On Saturday 1 October, at 8.30, she and her 13-year-old sister Alice stopped work and went for breakfast. As they were sat down, a boy named Robert Balderstone went past, and Ellen put her hands towards him. Balderstone shouted at her, 'I'll give it thee for that,' and got hold of her. They began struggling, and Ellen called out to her sister to help her. Just then the boy was seen to kick her in the abdomen and strike her with his fists in the chest. Ellen fell upon her knees, and the boy ran off. Ellen was still unconscious when she was carried into the mill yard, and there she died. She was conveyed to her home at Bolton Green, Charnock Richard. Balderstone was said to have been barefooted when he kicked Ellen, but unfortunately the deceased was not a strong child. The inquest into Ellen's death recorded a verdict of 'manslaughter' against Robert Balderstone, and that her death was caused by the shock produced on the nervous system by his blow.

2 OCTOBER   **1847**   An inquest was held before coroner Mr Molesworth at the Waggon & Horses Inn, Bury on the body of William Siddall, a grocer and mechanic of John Street. On 4 August, Siddall was visiting a factory at Unsworth on business; he got on one of the Manchester coaches with the intention of riding to Blackford Bridge. However, when the coach reached Blackford Bridge part of the road was paved, and the coach made such a clatter that the coachman could not hear the request to stop. Siddall attempted to get off the coach, but he became entangled and fell down, the coach dragging him a short distance and bruising him seriously about the head. He was taken to the Bridge Inn and medical help was procured. He lingered in great agony until death put an end to his suffering. The verdict was: 'Died from concussion of the brain caused by falling off a coach.'

3 OCTOBER   **1849**   Two farmers living in Formby, named Norris and Massam, had been drinking and began to quarrel, which eventually led to a fight. Both were advanced in years, and during the scuffle Norris fell backwards and died within a few hours. It appeared at the inquest that death was brought about by a fit, caused by passion and fighting. Massam, doubtless fearing a charge of manslaughter, attended the inquest regretting the fatal occurrence most emphatically, and concluded that as long as he lived he would never touch another drop of ale or spirits. The coroner lectured him on the evils of drink. After the verdict was returned Massam was overjoyed, and, in spite of his teetotal convictions and the satisfaction of escaping the verdict of 'manslaughter', he forgot all decorum and threw down a half crown for the jury – so they could all have a drink with him after court!

1874 Billy Woods, a fitter of Bridgeman Street, Bolton, went home after a day's heavy drinking in town and found that his front door was barred. In anger, he kicked the door in. When his wife came running downstairs to see what the matter was, he knocked her down and dragged her outside. Her mother, Ann Longshaw, went to protect her daughter – but she too was knocked to the ground. Woods then started to kick his mother-in-law viciously about the chest and legs, cracking one of her ribs. She was so severely hurt that Dr Patrick had to attend to her. Billy Woods was found guilty and sentenced to six months' hard labour.

4 OCTOBER

1895 Mr Walkden, a Blackburn pawnbroker, heard a burglar moving about downstairs in his shop early one morning. Arming himself with a pair of fire tongs, he went downstairs and confronted a man named John Barnes in the act of rifling the till. He challenged him, and a desperate struggle took place – the criminal swearing that he would murder Mr Walkden if he did not let him go. After fifteen minutes of fighting, Mr Walkden stunned the man, and afterwards handed him over to the police.

5 OCTOBER

1857 An inquest was held at the Bridge Inn, Padiham, on the body of Jonathan Clegg, a boatman who had died the previous Sunday morning about three hours after a quarrel with Miles Whittam, a blacksmith and neighbour. Whittam was taken into custody, and brought up at the Court House on Monday, but was remanded to await the outcome of the inquest. At the inquest it was stated that Clegg had returned home from Salterforth, Yorkshire, on Saturday night at ten o'clock. He took his horse as far as the foot of the bridge over the East Lancashire Railway. On the way he passed Whittam, who was standing at his door, intoxicated. Whittam followed Clegg, and asked him who had ordered him to take his horse up there. The deceased replied 'No one', upon which Whittam struck him on the cheek, and knocked him into a ditch at the side of the road. Whittam then put his hand between Clegg's neckerchief and his throat, but the neckerchief gave way. He was still standing over Clegg, when some women who had heard the commotion came and separated the men. As each man was led off, their bickering continued – but there was no more fighting. When Clegg got home he told the women he lodged with what had happened, and said that he felt very ill. He went to bed immediately, complaining of great pain and expressing his belief that he was about to die. He died at two o'clock on the Sunday morning. He had suffered from heart palpitations for about twelve months; a post-mortem examination revealed that disease of the heart had been the cause of death. The surgeon, Mr Dean of Padiham, said that the blow upon the cheek had not contributed to his death.

6 OCTOBER

7 OCTOBER   **1874** Patrick Flynn was charged with assaulting Police Constable Mathieson and a man named Matthew Day. Two days previous, the constable heard cries of 'Murder!' coming from Henaghan's lodging house on Water Street, Chorley. On arrival he found that Flynn had Matthew Day on the floor and was striking and kicking him about the head and legs. Flynn's wife took Mathieson's stick off him and struck the constable on the back with it, urging her husband to kill him. Flynn got hold of the constable's whiskers and kicked at him, but with some assistance the fellow was eventually taken into custody. Matthew Day stated that Flynn had knocked him down without provocation and had beaten and kicked him. In court, the magistrates found Flynn guilty of the assault and fined him 20s plus costs in each case, in default of fourteen days' imprisonment for each offence.

8 OCTOBER   **1825** The atrocious murder of an aged couple took place at a lonely farmhouse on the moors near Birtle-cum-Bamford, between Bury and Rochdale. A brother of the old couple had left them at about 10.30 p.m., after which the old woman had taken time to prepare for bed. The next morning they were both found brutally murdered. The man was sitting in his chair, his skull fractured; the woman was over him, as if trying to protect him from the savage blows – she too had succumbed to brutal injuries. There appeared to have been no motive for the crime; eight or ten shillings were still in place on a window sill in the farm cottage. About one o'clock on the same night, a man named John Diggle was seen nearby where some men were burning charcoal; he had with him a bundle of clothes. He stayed awhile at the charcoal pit and gave the men some cheese. To one of the men he sold two pairs of stockings, later found to have been taken from the farm where the murder had been committed. When Diggle was arrested, his clothes showed signs of being bloodstained. He implied that another man, Ralph West, was involved in the murder, but West appeared to have an alibi (it was confirmed that he was at Burnley at the time). The jury at the inquest returned a verdict of 'wilful murder' against Diggle. At his trial at the Lancaster Assizes on Thursday, 16 March 1826, he was found guilty of the despicable offence and sentenced to be hanged the following Monday. 'From the drop he fell and was launched into eternity – he appeared to struggle very little,' said the newspaper reports.

9 OCTOBER   **1848** James Illingworth and Henry Pilkington, two sturdy fellows, were brought up before the magistrates at Blackburn. That morning they had gone for relief at Mr Ashton's office, and were charged with throwing stones through the window at the relieving officer. The charge was proved by Mr Ashton and corroborated by PC Dowd. The defendants were convicted and fined 10s and costs with 3s 9d damages. In default they were committed to the house of correction for one month.

1832 There was a great deal of anger in Blackburn town over the 'improper' removal of gravestones from the old parish church there. One headstone was recently discovered being used as a 'useful domestic' in James's Street – whilst another had been taken up from its original location and repositioned near Livesey Street. A headstone which bore the inscription 'Mary Joice Rogerson' was discovered on Dandy Walk, fixed with iron bolts on one side of the bridge as a safeguard to prevent pedestrians falling into the brook there. It is known that Mrs Rogerson was interred within the old parish churchyard, for which privilege the sum of three guineas was paid, and the stone in question was placed over her at a time when the old church was being pulled down. Her son was very anxious that the spot where his mother had been laid to rest should remain marked – and to this end he gave the sexton a sum of 10s to lower the stone a little below the surface, and to resume its place above ground once all rubble from the old church had been removed. The three guineas were duly pocketed, as were the 10s, but the gravestone was still taken from the yard and used for an entirely different purpose.

10 OCTOBER

1849 A party of eleven men descended a new coal pit being sunk at Wigan and, on a scaffold lowered about 100 yards from the surface, sang a selection of anthems and psalms accompanied by Mr Wyseall on violin and Mr Adams on violoncello. After spending two pleasant hours, they safely ascended the shaft and afterwards adjourned to Messrs Crosses where dinner had been prepared for them.

11 OCTOBER

1895 For several weeks Richard Wilson had been living hermit-like on the shores of Morecambe Bay between Morecambe and Hest Bank. An enclosure of paling and sacking marked his territory. Here, with fire in a bucket, he did his own cooking and washing, sleeping at night beside his fire bucket. People in the district were in awe of the modern-day Crusoe. He was, however, brought before the magistrates and, on condition that he moved on, was dismissed from the courts.

12 OCTOBER

1849 Mary Ann Wright was charged by Mr Hugh Kershaw (the owner of the Star Hotel in Mount Pleasant, Oldham) with stealing a pocket handkerchief and a woollen shawl. Wright had been living with Kershaw as a servant, and when he suspected her of theft he discharged her – after which the aforementioned articles went missing. This information was given to the police and a search was made; the missing property was found in her possession. About £4 in cash was

13 OCTOBER

also found stitched into the lining of her boots. The articles being identified, Wright was committed for trial.

14 OCTOBER **1992** Having built the very foundation of the Industrial Revolution, and fuelled the fires and steam engines that 'made Britain great', the coal miner was later cast aside. The coal mines of Lancashire and other parts of the country were closed down, ending an industry second only to agriculture in antiquity. For generations past, father worked alongside son, brother by brother, in the Lancashire coal mines. The great tradition ended in 1992 when the government announced its 'Plan for Coal'. This plan included the closure of practically all of the nation's collieries, and the redundancy of tens of thousands of miners – all forsaken for the price of cheap imported coal, often hewed with the labour of children.

Expendable!
The pit stands dead, the wheels are still
There's no more coal for the men to fill
Machinery stands there rusted and broke
The blackened chimney emits no smoke.

The young men have gone to different mines,
But for men like Jack, it's just hard lines.
A lifetime of knowledge, his views respected
But they say he's too old, he's been rejected.

No more for Jack the pit cage's swift drop,
The air's cool roar as they leave the top,
Or the ribald jesting with his mates,
On the paddy ride to the different gates.

No more will Jack duck into the face,
With a practised glance as he takes his place.
And pits his strength, and his wit and skill
At the daily task that can maim and kill.

He pretends not to care, he's done with the pit.
He's had a bellyful, to hell with it.
But he feels half a man, as he sees his friends
When they take the bus at four lane ends.

He stands there forlorn, he doesn't feel old,
But they've written him off, he's out in the cold,
Bereft of his living and a way of life

He wanders aimless home to his patient wife.

[Poet unknown]

1860 A 20-year-old woman named Beck, a native of Lancaster, was apprehended on a charge of stealing the 14-week-old daughter of Thomas Taylor of Little Bolton. When apprehended, the prisoner was leaving Lancaster for the north; the child was found in a field, where the prisoner had left it knowing the police were on her track. The object of obtaining the child was to help her while she was out begging, and the infant appeared to have suffered much in the absence of its parents. The prisoner had nothing to say in her defence and was committed to the Lancaster Assizes for sentence.

1851 A fatal accident occurred at Pendlebury, Manchester, through the incautious use of gunpowder. Sarah Musgrove kept a small shop across from the Royal Oak Inn for the sale of drapery, groceries and gunpowder. She had been selling 6lb of gunpowder to a collier, and soon afterwards 16lb of gunpowder in three small vessels exploded. The house and shop of Sarah Musgrove were destroyed, along with a newly-built cottage alongside. Mrs Musgrove was discovered in the ruins, as were her 7-year-old and 1-year-old children, who were much burnt. Mrs Musgrove was removed to the Royal Oak, where she died on the following Monday afternoon.

The Royal Oak, where Sarah Musgrove died following the explosion of gunpowder in her shop.

17 OCTOBER   **1826**   The captain of the smack *Latuna*, in George's Dock Passage, Liverpool, investigated an unpleasant smell coming from three casks which had been delivered from a cart the previous day; he found that they contained human bodies in dry salt. A constable was sent for and in one cask was found one male and two female bodies, in the second two male and two females, and in the third three males and one female. The casks, with their contents, were taken to the dead house in Chapel Street. The carter said he had brought the casks from a cellar under the school room of the Revd J. M'Gowan in Hope Street. The constable proceeded to the school room, and, having broken into it, found three casks and three sacks containing the bodies of nine men, five women, five boys and three girls. An inquiry was held before the coroner. It appeared that a man named Henderson had occupied the cellar for nearly a year and was supposed to be in the oil trade. The first three casks were directed to Mr G.H. Ironson, Edinburgh, and were labelled 'Bitter salts'. A surgeon stated that the bodies in the cask appeared to have been there for about six or seven days, but those in the sacks only two or three days. They were all interred on the following Tuesday.

18 OCTOBER   **1882**   An hour before midnight, near the corner of Cornhill, Liverpool, Thomas Walsh heard a scream. On investigation he found a woman lying on the ground; running away was someone dressed like a sailor. Walsh pursued the man but soon lost him, and returned to the female. A passing stranger offered assistance and the police were soon at hand – and the girl was taken to hospital. She was seriously injured on the head and face, and, after remaining unconscious until 2.30 a.m., the poor girl died. Later, a French sailor named Auguste Forestier was arrested and charged with the manslaughter of the girl, now named as Ann Jane Oliver, who he alleged was trying to steal his watch. At his trial in November he was acquitted of the crime.

MURDER AT LIVERPOOL

Thomas Walsh, at the scene of the murder, watches the shadowy figure of a sailor disappear into the night.

1892   The body of a woman who had not been seen for seven weeks was discovered underneath the stairs at 412 Hollins Road, Oldham.

The discovery was made by the landlord who, upon looking through the window, saw that the stone flags inside had been removed and there was an open grave beside a pile of earth. The police searched the property and found the woman wrapped up in a carpet full of blood, and her body badly decomposed – the head had been severed from the body with a knife, which was found on the floor of the house, and there were many stab wounds to the breast. Close by was a barrel of quick-lime, which apparently was going to be thrown into the grave. The victim was the wife of Joseph Mellor, a winder at Osborne Mills not more than 2 miles away from the house. Joseph

The murder at Hollins Road, Oldham, in 1892.

Mellor was quickly arrested at his place of work and charged with the grim act, to which he made no reply. After the inquest into his wife's murder, Mellor had to be led from the court laughing in a very strange way and acting extremely callously. In late November, Joseph Mellor was sentenced to death at Manchester Assizes.

1869   A fatal boiler explosion occurred at Mr Bramley's Foundry in Accrington; two people perished. Those killed were John Cass aged 67, and Lawrence Howarth aged 14. The inquest put the cause of the explosion down to corrosion of the plates at the seat of the boiler. There was also want of care on the part of those in charge, in not following up the indications of dampness.

1895   Sixty-year-old Maria Moran of Davy Street, Barrowford, was found dead in her bed, and an inquest into her demise was held on this day. A neighbour became concerned, having not seen Maria for some days, and summoned the police to her house. The police broke into the property and found the woman lying on her bed; it appears that she had been dead for around a fortnight. Dr Pim stated that death was by natural causes, probably accelerated by want – a verdict to this effect was recorded.

1877   Shortly before six o'clock, an explosion occurred at the Rake Head Mill at Burnley with loss of life. About six weeks previous, a

The damage to Rake Head Mill following the fatal boiler explosion in 1877.

new engine was put into the mill, the steam being conveyed from the old boiler house across to the new engine in a large pipe. The engine tenter, Michael Mulloy, along with his assistant George Johnstone, was turning on the steam through the pipe to allow the engine to warm up when the pipe burst. Both operatives were blown across the engine room and were dreadfully scalded – Johnstone died within a few hours of the explosion, and Mulloy, although seriously burnt, was expected to recover. A great deal of damage was done to the engine house.

23 OCTOBER   **1833**   A tame starling belonging to Mr Hartley of the Star Inn, John Street, Preston – which had been taught to whistle, call the dog, and imitate the ringing of bells – was often released from its cage. On 23 October 1833, however, it escaped out of the front door and flew away. The following morning, Mr Hartley was out walking his dog through the fields when to his astonishment the bird came to him, sat on a fence, and began calling – but evaded all attempts to recapture it. The bird flew over the field and into a plantation, the owner calling in vain, and then the dog also ran off. When he approached them, he found the bird sitting close to the dog, and after a few attempts both were recaptured and returned home.

24 OCTOBER   **1854**   An inquest was held at the Rostron Arms in Edenfield touching the death of Sampson Knight, aged 22, who was drowned under a gasometer. It appeared that James Rostron wanted to restart Dearden Clough Mill, which had been standing for seventeen years, and he also wanted to bring the gasometer back into use. However, one of the gas pipes appeared to be blocked and Knight volunteered to make a raft and go under the gasometer to unblock it. After a short time nothing was heard from Knight, in spite of Mr Rostron calling out to him. It was assumed that he might have fallen off the raft and got into trouble inside the gasometer. A rescue operation was put into effect, but it was many hours before the dead body of Sampson Knight was recovered. The jury returned a verdict of 'accidental death'.

25 OCTOBER   **1878**   James Alston, a gamekeeper of Broughton Lane, Woodplumpton, was charged at Preston Police Court with attempting to murder William

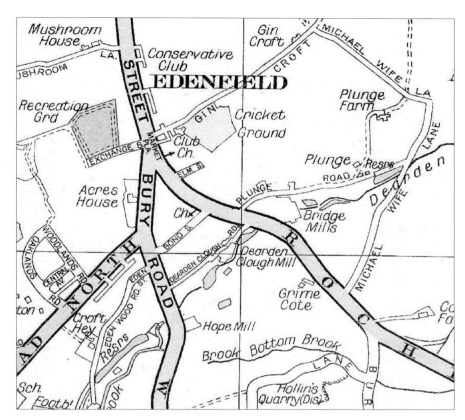

The Dearden Clough Mill, where Sampson Knight met his death in 1854, can be seen on this 1930s' map.

Gregory. On 24 July, Alston's son told John Irvin, a former policeman, that a man had been shot. Irvin set off to see James Alston – who admitted that he had shot someone in his garden. He said that he had heard a noise in the hen cote and, seeing somebody there, had run downstairs with a gun in his hands. As he approached the cote he called out, 'Stop or I will fire!' He got no answer so he fired – the man, William Gregory, then ran off, later turning up at Billington's Farm. Alston went there and searched Gregory but found no evidence of game, hens or pheasant about him. As to his injuries, Gregory stated that he had been trod upon by a horse – however, these wounds were so serious that he had to have his leg amputated a few days later. The court, after some deliberation, committed James Alston to the Liverpool Assizes for trial. On 5 February 1879, he appeared before the Assizes, and Alston was acquitted of the charge – the judge, however, added this: 'You may leave the dock, but take my advice and don't shoot at people carelessly in your garden again. Had you killed this man you would have been in serious trouble.'

1869 Westhoughton was the scene of a murder and a suicide. Henry Whittle, a 47-year-old weaver, murdered his 24-year-old daughter- 26 OCTOBER in-law Ellen Whittle with a hatchet, and then cut his own throat. The murderer lived with his son Roger, a collier at Chapel Walk, but had been unhappy since his son had married Ellen. In fact, he once threatened to kill both Roger and Ellen – and was told to leave the house. Arguments arose over the ownership of pieces of furniture, which caused even greater animosity between the trio. Roger left for work on 26 October, leaving his father and Ellen alone in the house. At about 10.30 a.m., Ellen's mother came to the house to help her daughter do some cleaning, but the front door was locked. Peering through the window, she was horrified to see her daughter lying in a pool of blood. When the police arrived they found Henry on a bed in the back bedroom, also dead.

27 OCTOBER **1871** Thomas Davies and his wife Ann were found dead in their beds at Ladygate Lane, Breightmet. It appeared that the husband, in a fit of insanity, had tried to shoot his wife during the night with a pistol. The cap, however, did not explode, and so he strangled her. He then took his own life by cutting his throat. A verdict to this effect was returned at the inquest.

SHOCKING MURDER & SUICIDE AT BREIGHMET

Thomas Davies murdered his wife before cutting his own throat in 1871.

28 OCTOBER **1893** It was said – probably without foundation – that Caroline Harriet Tyrer, aged 77, had lots of money stacked away at her house in Salford. This came to the attention of 25-year-old Emmanuel Hamer, who was working with other men painting the houses outside. On this day he paid a visit to Caroline. Mr and Mrs Denson, who lived next door, heard someone talking to the lady and then heard a bump. They went to investigate; the house was in darkness and a voice called out, 'You are not coming into my house!' Mrs Denson replied, 'But I want to see Mrs Tyrer.' The reply was, 'You can't see her; you can't come into my house.' Meanwhile Mr Denson, who had gone to the rear of

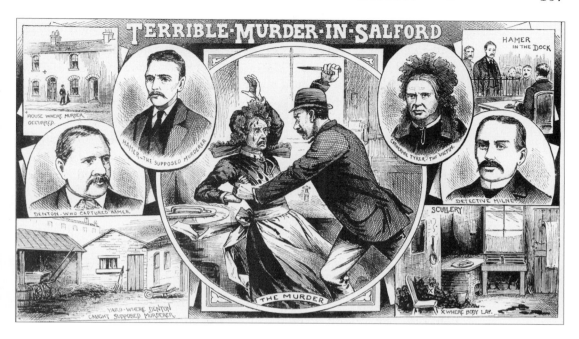

the house, saw and recognised Hamer coming out of the back door. Mr Denson gave chase and caught the man. Hamer was arrested and Mrs Tyrer was found in her kitchen with her skull smashed in – she died the following Sunday.

The events that led to the terrible murder of old Mrs Tyrer.

1894 The Lancaster coroner held an inquest at Caton into the death of Agnes Elizabeth Wildman, aged 17, who for just three weeks had been employed at the Ship Inn, kept by Mrs Wilkinson. The previous Thursday the girl had been found in an apparent state of intoxication, and was scolded by her mistress and her mother, the latter having struck her. The next morning she rose early – about four o'clock – but was sent to bed again. An hour later she got up again, and asked for the keys of the cellar and bar to enable her to clean up. Mrs Wilkinson refused to let her have them, and in another hour the girl was again found apparently drunk and unconscious. She was taken home and found to be full of carbolic acid. When she came round she told the police that she had taken it because she was accused of being drunk – she also said that she was tired of life. She died on the Saturday night. A verdict of 'committed suicide whilst temporarily insane' was recorded.

29 OCTOBER

1858 Reports were made on the death of John Mansergh Askew, the corn miller at Kirkby, Lonsdale; the inquest was held at the Royal Hotel there. After dinner, the deceased had started the mill; his wife, noticing that it had stopped about ten minutes later, went to see what was

30 OCTOBER

wrong. She called out but got no answer and, on ascending the stairs, saw her husband under the grinding wheels. His body was between the fly wheel and the jack wheel; his arms were hanging over the wheels, and his right shoulder and the right side of his chest were held fast between the cogwheels. His wife ran down and turned off the water, then went for help. With the aid of a neighbour she released him, but he was quite dead. The jury returned a verdict according to the facts.

31 OCTOBER   1845   A 72-year-old man named John Boram, a former inn keeper at Colne and lately a journeyman saddler at Preston, was found hanged by the neck off one of the rafters in an outbuilding of the Market House in Burnley. How long he had been hanging there was unknown, but it was thought to have been several hours. The body was removed to the Market Tavern to await an inquest.

NOVEMBER

Moorfield Colliery Disaster

This memorial is dedicated to the 68 men and boys who tragically lost their lives in the Moorfield Colliery Disaster on the morning of Wednesday 7th November 1883

NAME		AGE	NAME		AGE	NAME		AGE
Almond, Cuthbert	✝	12	Grimshaw, John	✝	20	Riley, Robert	✝	17
Almond, John	✝	20	Grimshaw, Thomas	✝	26	Rushton, John	✝	27
Alston, Thomas	✝	16	Gumm, William	✝	26	Rushton, Lawrence	✝	27
Ashworth, James	✝	39	Hall, John Thomas	✝	15	Rushton, Robert	✝	44
Atherton, James	✝	10	Hamriding, Thomas	✝	36	Rushton, William	✝	14
Bentley, John	✝	32	Haworth, Job Whittaker	✝	11	Scholes, James	✝	19
Blackburn, Thomas	✝	23	Haworth, Robert	✝	36	Shorrock, John	✝	19
Broadley, James	✝	40	Haworth, Rothwell	✝	34	Smith, John Edward	✝	11
Broadley, Westwell	✝	28	Haworth, William Henry	✝	32	Smith, Thomas	✝	45
Brown, Waddington Walter	✝	23	Hollin, William	✝	25	Tapper, George	✝	18
Clegg, George	✝	18	Jones, William Edward	✝	13	Taylor, James	✝	35
Clegg, Henry William	✝	19	Leeson, Joseph	✝	12	Taylor, Thomas	✝	29
Clough, James	✝	27	Macintosh, Thomas	✝	56	Taylor William	✝	24
Clough, Steven	✝	19	Macintosh, Thomas Henry	✝	35	Taylor, Wilson	✝	29
Coles, Walter Henry	✝	32	Mackrell, William	✝	21	Thornton, Joseph	✝	24
Crabb, John	✝	40	Mahon, John	✝	15	Threlfall, John	✝	46
Cronshaw, Jackson	✝	21	Mahon, Michael	✝	13	Threlfall, Robert	✝	25
Cronshaw, James	✝	27	Metcalf, Thomas	✝	33	Tillotson, Thomas	✝	28
Cronshaw, Thomas	✝	25	Osbaldeston, James	✝	37	Tomlinson, Peter	✝	19
Crossley, Henry	✝	11	Osbaldeston, Richard	✝	12	Walsh, Thomas	✝	27
Edge, John	✝	16	Ormerod, John	✝	41	Yates, Timothy	✝	29
Edge, Thomas	✝	14	Perry, Mathew Henry	✝	17	Yates, William	✝	46
Gorton, Robert	✝	30	Riding, Aaron	✝	10			

A memorial card to those who perished in the Moorfield Colliery disaster, 7 November 1883.

1 NOVEMBER   **1840**   A young man named Edward Riley, a fisherman of Knott End, met with a premature death whilst out fishing. He was in the boat when the boom caught him and knocked him overboard. He sank and immediately rose again but no assistance could be rendered, even though his brother was a short distance from the spot. After a brief struggle, he again sank without a shriek at the mouth of the river Wyre; it was conjectured that his body drifted out to sea. He left a widow and child to mourn his loss.

2 NOVEMBER   **1876**   At Fleetwood Police Court, Isabella Whiteside was charged with causing the death of her new-born baby. Dr Aspinall's opinion was that the cause of death was strangulation, whilst Dr Porter thought it was congestion of the brain. The Bench came to the conclusion that there was no evidence of murder, manslaughter or concealment of birth, and the girl was discharged.

3 NOVEMBER   **1924**   A rail disaster occurred at Lytham on the Fylde Coast when the train was derailed at a crossing; it then hit a bridge and the Warton signal box, which it completely demolished. The coals from the engine also set fire to one of the carriages. The scene of the accident – about a mile outside Lytham – was an isolated place, and, during the rescue, bonfires had to be lit to illuminate the scene on this cold winter's evening. The train was used nightly by the mill girls working at Kirkham. The total number of fatalities reached fourteen, with many others injured.

4 NOVEMBER   **1852**   Boggart Hole in Clough lies near Blackley in Manchester – its name tells us that it was once, or perhaps still is, thought to be the home of boggarts, the northern fairy. It has been many years now since boggarts were last seen here; the last time appears to have been in 1852, when they decided to flit to Blackley Village itself. The house they chose to visit was a very old building adjoining the White Lion, occupied by a clogger named William Whitehead. When he first heard the boggarts they made a sound like the cackling of an old hen, or a train whistle – and if any of the family stood upon a certain flag in the back room it screamed like a child having a tantrum. Whitehead removed the flag and dug a hole several feet deep; he came across a cream jug filled with lime and bones. The old folks of the village declared that these were the remnants of 'Old Shaw's Wife'; Shaw was a former resident of the Old Hall, which used to stand close by. One boggart was heard every night of the week, and sometimes during the day. It made a greater noise than usual one night, and Whitehead spent the next day digging for the supposed spirit. An old man named George Horrox, who used to live in the dwelling, stated that on two occasions he had seen a ghost in the shape of a woman, and she had made a rumbling noise. Other elders of the village claimed that the house had been haunted for the past eighty years. The news about the haunting spread, and the publicans of the village appear to have done a roaring trade as outsiders came to see the place where the boggarts roamed.

1877 George Pigott was a 29-year-old miner at one of the coal mines at Kearsley, just outside Bolton. He was married and had several children – but he also had a mistress, Florence Galloway. She had known Pigott since she was a child and eventually he persuaded her to live with him as man and wife. They settled down in a small cottage in Birmingham. But the union did not last, and, on 5 November 1877, Florence returned to her mother's house. Amazingly, George returned to his wife and family, who seemed quite willing to take him back, but he was still infatuated with Florence and tried everything to get back with her. Her mother was having none of it – she refused point blank to let Pigott have any further dealings with her daughter. Pigott then devised a plan. He wrote a letter to Florence's mother which purported to come from a friend of theirs, a Mrs Wilson, and it contained news that Mrs Wilson had a job for both mother and daughter. As they left the house on 5 November to go to Mrs Wilson's, George Pigott confronted them in the street. Mrs Galloway was furious at being duped, and told Pigott that he was never going to see Florence again. 'So be it,' replied George, and taking a step back pulled a pistol from his pocket and shot Florence through the head. She was fatally wounded and fell to the ground – the deed had been done. Pigott was arrested and charged with wilful murder. His defence claimed that he had no intention of killing Florence, and that the weapon was carried to enable him to take his own life if he was not able to see Florence again – and the gun had simply gone off accidentally. Members of the jury, however, were not convinced and took just half an hour to return with a verdict of guilty. The judge donned his black cap and passed the death sentence upon George Pigott.

1892 Reports were coming in of yet another murder at Oldham. The victim was the stepsister of James Jackson who, after committing his brutal act, turned the razor upon himself and committed suicide. At the inquest, the mother of both told how her son had often threatened to murder the girl, and while he was serving in

How the *Illustrated Police News* showed the savage murder at Oldham, and the subsequent suicide of the murderer.

India he had suffered from sunstroke. He had also attempted to hang himself in recent times. The jury found Jackson guilty of murder and then committing suicide while insane. Other reports stated that Jackson had been unduly intimate with his stepsister, resulting in the birth of a child.

7 NOVEMBER   **1883**   East Lancashire's worst mining disaster occurred at the Moorfield Colliery at Altham, near Clayton-le-Moors, when an underground explosion wiped out the lives of sixty-eight men and boys. Many of the victims were school-aged children – and hardly a neighbour wasn't affected in some way by the disaster. A widow, Mrs Almond, lost two sons that day – John aged 20, and Cuthbert who was just 12 years old. Another son, George, died as an indirect result; he was badly burnt in the blast and died in May the following year whilst having a tooth extracted – through an overdose of chloroform. Another family had unbelievable bad luck in their lives. David Cronshaw had to identify his three sons, Jackson, James and Thomas, who were killed in the explosion – a fourth son was badly injured. The family already had a son killed previously in the pit, and another son was drowned in the canal; the previous year their daughter Jane had died. James Clegg volunteered to help clean up the bodies of the victims in preparation for burial, and failed to notice his own son, William, who had been badly burned. The family also lost another son in the blast, and the mother, Mrs Clegg, lost two brothers. Eleven-year-old Henry Crossley died on his third day at the pit. Thirteen-year-old Michael Mahon was actually making his way out of the pit when he turned round and went back for his brother, 15-year-old John

In more recent years, this fine memorial to those who perished at the Moorfield Colliery in November 1883 has been erected near what would have been the entrance to the colliery. A fitting tribute to East Lancashire's worst mining disaster.

– both were later found dead. Other pitiful scenes and brave actions included the death of 14-year-old Thomas Edge, who was carried out of the underground hell by his father, only to die three days later. His brother John, aged 16, also perished. Another hero that day was James Macintosh, the under-manager at the pit; he was one of the first down and spent the next twenty-four hours searching for the dead and injured – the dead included his father Thomas, the manager of the colliery. James never again went down the pit – he became landlord of the Greyhound Inn just down the road. On the tenth anniversary of the disaster, he came into the public bar out of hours and committed suicide by slashing his throat with a razor.

1892 Nine-year-old Alice Barnes was found dead, suffocated by a handkerchief in Witton Park, Blackburn. The murderer had bared her legs and tampered with her clothing, but hadn't actually interfered with her sexually. The cause of death was an unusual handkerchief stuffed down her throat. The police took an interest in 32-year-old Cross Duckworth when he started talking about the murder in several of the local inns. They arrested him on suspicion and, on searching his home, found a number of handkerchiefs all identical to the one used to suffocate poor Alice. Duckworth constantly protested his innocence, but at his two-day trial he was unable to explain the presence of the handkerchiefs at his house. He was found guilty of the vile offence and sentenced to death; he was hanged at Walton Prison, Liverpool on Tuesday, 3 January 1893.

8 NOVEMBER

The death cell where Cross Duckworth waited to be hanged for the murder of Alice Barnes.

1838 High on Winter Hill, near Horwich, around 800 yards from the TV mast and among the heath land, is a simple memorial erected in memory of George Henderson who was murdered at that spot in 1838. Locally this is known as 'Scotsman's Stump'. George Henderson was employed by a draper in Blackburn; his job was to travel around the neighbourhood collecting and delivering orders. It was usual for him to report back to the draper at Blackburn every Friday, and on this particular occasion his route was from Blackrod, over Winter Hill down to Belmont village and thence to Blackburn. It is known that George lodged the night at the Old Cock Inn, Blackrod, and it was from there

9 NOVEMBER

'Scotsman's Stump' marks the spot of a fatal shooting which happened in 1838. It bears the inscription: 'In memory of George Henderson, traveller, native of Annan, Dumfriesshire, who was brutally murdered on Rivington Moor at noonday, November 9th, 1838, in the 20th year of his age.' (Jack Nadin)

that he set off towards the mist-covered moors – it was also the last time that he was seen alive. Around 12.15 p.m. shots were heard, and a youth passing close by went to investigate. Seeing blood and a body in the ditch, the young lad ran for help at one of the coal mines on the moor. They found Henderson lying on his back with a shotgun wound through the head. He was removed to a group of buildings on the moors known as 'Garbutt's', but he died there at around 2.30 p.m. A local man, James Whittle, had been seen on the moors with a gun – he was the prime suspect of the murder. After further investigation he was arrested, charged with wilful murder, and committed to Kirkdale Prison for trial at Liverpool. However, after an extensive hearing Whittle was acquitted of all charges, and to this day the person, or persons, responsible for taking the life of George Henderson is unknown. The simple memorial was placed there in 1912 as a reminder of the horrific events so many years ago.

10 NOVEMBER **1862** Anne Walne, aged 80, had lived at the Setter's Arms, near Ribchester, for thirty-three years as a beer seller and farmer of a little acreage. As November 1862 approached she realised that her rent would be due, and in order to pay this she sold off one of her cows. Some local criminals got wind of this and decided that they could make better use of the rent money. The men were Duncan McPhail, Benjamin Hartley, Daniel Carr and George Woods. On 10 November, a wild and stormy night, they left Blackburn at 6 a.m. Reaching Ribchester around eight o'clock, and crossing the fields, they rested in a barn. They then waited in some hedgerows until two o'clock, when McPhail gave the word, and the foursome moved towards the Setter's Arms. They gained entry through one of the windows and confronted Anne, demanding to know where the money was stashed. Anne refused to say, and started to shout out; one of the robbers struck her violently – fatally, as it happened. The robber fled. A reward of £100 proved too much for Benjamin Hartley; he turned Queen's Evidence and betrayed his companions. The three were arrested but Carr died in prison, or, according to local tradition, drowned himself in a water closet. McPhail and Woods were sentenced to death and hanged at Kirkdale Prison on 25 April 1863 before a crowd of 40,000. Hartley had to leave his home at Blackburn because the local mill operatives refused to work with him, and he disappeared into oblivion.

The Setter's Arms, where Anne Walne was murdered in 1862, has today been converted into a farmhouse and cottage.

In 1957, a Mr William Barton wrote that his father was raised by the murdered woman and used to look after her stock. On the day of the murder, he was returning from Blackburn where he had been delivering some hay, and, as he approached the inn with her money, saw what he thought were a couple of poachers. On entering the house he found the old woman dead. It seems that the robbers never found the money, because it was still in Mr Barton's father's pocket at the time.

1861 An inquest was held at Carnforth upon the body of Robert Caley, a farmer of Town End who was found hanged at his own farm on the previous Saturday. It appeared that the deceased had been in low spirits since a girl with whom he had been keeping company had deserted him. On the day in question, Caley went to bed for an hour or two, saying that he had had very little sleep during the night; he rose at about 1.30 p.m. He went out of the house, and, as he was passing the window, his sister called out to him that dinner was ready. He called back to say that he would be in shortly, but he did not return. At about two o'clock, his brother William went into the stable and found him hanging by his neck by a plough cord. His brother lifted him up and cut the cord, but Caley was quite dead. It was stated at the inquest: 'The object of his misplaced affection was still unmarried.' The verdict of the inquest jury was 'temporary insanity'.

11 NOVEMBER

1872 James Carr was charged with stabbing Joshua Gent at Preston Police Court. On the previous Saturday at around 12.30 in the afternoon,

12 NOVEMBER

The stabbing of Joshua Gent in 1872 later proved to be fatal.

the two men were in a lodging house in Lancaster Road, Preston, when a third man named Parker came in. The men began a rough game known as a 'Bull Fight', which consisted of the parties slapping each other's faces. When Carr had received a slap or two he exclaimed, 'I'll show you!' and suddenly stabbed Gent in the right eye with a clasp knife with which he had been eating his food. The injured man was taken to the Infirmary, where he remained in an unstable condition. Carr was remanded, and Gent later died from his injuries. In December, Carr appeared on a charge of manslaughter at the Sessions and was sentenced to four months' imprisonment.

13 NOVEMBER **1857** Robert Riley, a 21-year-old spindle maker, was at work at the premises of Charles Baldwin & Baron in Calder Street, Burnley. His occupation was to grind spindles using a wheel – on this particular day using a wheel which was just a few days old. Grinding wheels were notorious for 'bursting', and because of this the wheel was being run at what was called 'first' or 'slow' speed (about 660 revolutions per minute). The normal speed was between 700 and 800 revolutions per minute. The other workers were alarmed to hear a loud crack, and Robert Riley was found lying on the floor on his back. The grindstone had burst, and a portion of the stone had embedded itself in the side of Riley's head. 'He was bleeding very much, the skull was fractured from the eye to the back of the head – and he was quite dead,' said a witness at the inquest, held at the Commercial Inn in Cheapside the following day. A verdict of 'accidental death' was recorded.

14 NOVEMBER **1859** An inquest was held at the Dog & Partridge inn, Hesketh Lane, Chipping village, touching on the death of 18-year-old Richard Proctor. The deceased worked for Henry Bleasdale & Sons, machine makers at Chipping. He was seen by one of the workers on the previous Friday tangled in the machinery. The engine was stopped but the poor fellow was already dead and his body presented a shocking sight. His arms, thighs and legs were fearfully crushed and mangled, and some of his bones protruded from his legs. A verdict of 'accidental death' was recorded.

1890   After being missing for almost a week, schoolteacher Elizabeth Holt was found dead by one of her pupils on Longworth Lane, near Belmont village, to the north of Bolton. She had been brutally beaten, raped, kicked and bruised – but the cause of her death was a gaping gash across her throat. Suspicion was quickly aimed at Thomas MacDonald, a 32-year-old man with a previous record of rape. He was convicted of the depraved and vile offence at court, and on Tuesday, 30 December 1890 was hanged at Kirkdale Prison.

15 NOVEMBER

How the *Illustrated Police News* depicted the brutal murder of Elizabeth Holt in 1890.

1943   A Wellington Bomber took off from Wymeswold in Leicestershire. The plane contained six crew members: pilot Flight Sergeant Joseph Timperton, Eric Barnes, Joseph Hayton, Robert Jackson, Matthew Mouncy, and George Murray. As the aircraft flew low over the Pennines in Lancashire, the plane began to get into difficulties. The engines screamed out as Flight Sergeant Timperton wrestled with the controls, but it was in vain – the great bulk of the aircraft ploughed into the hillside on Hurst Hill, high on Anglezarke Moor near Chorley. All of the crew members were killed in the crash; the wreckage scattered over a large area. The investigation that followed concluded that the probable cause of the accident was 'loss of control, possibly due to ice which may have led to structural failure as the aircraft went into a high speed dive'. Each year on Remembrance Sunday a poignant service is held, high on the moors,

16 NOVEMBER

to those who perished. A memorial records the names of the men who died that day.

17 NOVEMBER **1848** The little village of Lees in Oldham was thrown into a state of alarm when a fire was discovered at the mills of Messrs John Andrews & Sons, County End Mills. The village fire engine was promptly on the scene, but it was found to be out of repair and quite inadequate to stop the progress of the flames. Messages were dispatched for the engine at Mumps Brook and for the *West of England* engine from Oldham. No time was lost in getting them to the scene, but an hour had elapsed before this could be accomplished. During this time the fire had got such a hold of the mill that it was beyond saving. Upwards of 300 people were thrown of employment by the calamity.

18 NOVEMBER **1887** There was a quarry accident at Chatburn near Clitheroe. John Driver, a man aged about 50, was working in Bold Venture Quarry as a stone breaker. Blasting operations were going on and a large piece of rock fell to the bottom of the quarry; a fragment broke off and struck Driver on the arm, breaking it just below the elbow.

19 NOVEMBER **1850** A fatal accident occurred to a man named John Collinge, employed at Mr Banks' brick and pot makers, at Windy Bank in the Forest of Rossendale. Collinge was returning home with his cart, intoxicated and asleep, when the cart hit a brick wall. It threw him out and passed over him. A young lad ran to the brickworks to get help. Collinge was released but only lingered in agony for a day or so before death put an end to his sufferings. An inquest, held at the Hargreaves Arms at Lumb, returned a verdict of 'accidental death'.

20 NOVEMBER **1856** There was an explosion at a small colliery named Town House Pit in Marsden (now Nelson, East Lancashire), caused by a man named William Critchley, who was attempting to fire a shot by taking off the top of his flame safety lamp. The shots should have been fired by the underlooker or the fireman, and not by the ordinary collier. Locked safety lamps were used at the colliery, and these had been examined prior to the men being allowed underground. It was stated that the 'German' – a lighted paper filled with gunpowder by which the shot was fired – was not properly fastened in the hole, and on being lit flew into the old workings and ignited the firedamp. Ten people were injured and three men were killed by the blast.

21 NOVEMBER **1834** The dangers of coal mining were again brought to the public's attention when there was an inundation at the Lomax Wood pit near

Bury. Twenty-three men and boys were in the pit when one of the miners hewing the coal pierced into some old workings with his pick. Immediately, hundreds of thousands of gallons of water rushed into the workings; men, wagons, tools and stones were carried along by the force of the water. The man who had caused the inrush clung on to a pit prop and hung there for three hours – naked, wet and cold. Had he let go he would have been dashed along the workings and almost certainly ended up dead. Six other men were driven out to the mouth of the pit, and the remaining men seemed destined to die. The inrush of water was slowly draining off through an inclined tunnel which was only driven a short time previous, and rescuers began to enter the mine to look for survivors. The tunnels were blocked with stones and water, but they came across one man who had managed to keep his nostrils above the water and he was dragged out of the mine. Soon others were extricated the same way, and by the end of the day all those who had been underground were rescued.

1843 A dreadful accident occurred to 11-year-old Christopher Greenwood, a piecer in the cotton mill of Mr White of Higher Booth (Rossendale). The lad was taking a strap off a pulley, when he pulled it too far and caused it to gather up. It caught his clothes and took him round the shafting, striking him repeatedly against the roof. When the engine was stopped he dropped to the floor, dead. An inquest recorded a verdict of 'accidental death'.

22 NOVEMBER

1874 George Nuttall, a weaver residing at Huncoat near Accrington, committed suicide by cutting his throat with a razor. The deceased was 34 years old and had been in low spirits for some time. His wife went for some milk at eight o'clock, and when she returned twenty minutes later she found her husband in the back yard with his throat cut and the razor in his hand. Notwithstanding medical assistance, he only survived two hours.

23 NOVEMBER

1884 Kay Howarth, a 25-year-old layabout, was hanged at Strangeways Prison for the murder of commercial traveller Richard Dugdale. On 3 October 1884, 37-year-old Dugdale left his hometown of Wakefield in Yorkshire to go about his business with town centre publicans in Bolton. In one of the public houses, he came across his old friend Robert Hall. The pair went for a meal and a drink, and were soon joined by a well-known local rogue, Kay Howarth. Robert Hall tried to ignore Howarth, but the latter was not to be put off, especially as he could see that Dugdale was carrying large amounts of cash. The trio went on an all-day drinking session, and by 6.30 p.m. Hall had to leave due to another appointment

24 NOVEMBER

– but before leaving, he insisted that Howarth take Dugdale back to the Wheatsheaf Hotel, where he had booked a room. Howarth agreed, and the pair were seen heading off towards the pub. Later that night, on waste ground near Silverwell Street, a man stumbled across the dead body of Richard Dugdale – he was cut about the throat and had a large gash on the back of his head. In Dugdale's hand was a knife, and beside him was a suicide note. It was soon obvious that this was not a case of suicide and, following enquiries, the police went to Howarth's house. They found him in bed, still covered in blood. A number of cheques and a gold watch and chain which belonged to Dugdale were also discovered in the house. At his trial in November he denied the charge of murder, but after a short deliberation the jury found him guilty. Dugdale left a wife, two sons and two daughters to mourn his loss.

25 NOVEMBER   1900   The *Illustrated Police News* reported:

> There has just died at Royton near Oldham an Irish woman named Keneally who is believed to have lived 110 years. She has resided in her later years with a daughter, aged 73 who was the youngest of thirteen children, and those who knew the deceased some years ago stated that some of her reminisces dated back as far as three years before the opening of the present century. She came from the west of Ireland thirty years ago, and had been blind for ten years. She was childish and bedridden during the last three or four years of her life.

26 NOVEMBER   1845   The *Manchester Guardian* reported:

> On Monday last at the Borough Court, Margaret Greenhalgh, wife of Mr Greenhalgh, shopkeeper, Blackburn Street, Little Bolton was summoned by Elizabeth Rothwell for wilfully damaging a silk dress. The circumstances are these. On Saturday week, the house of James Rothwell was blown up by an explosion of gunpowder, by which his son was killed and his furniture destroyed. The women of the neighbourhood searched among the ruins for what property they could find, and discovered a silk dress, which they took to Mrs Greenhalgh for security. She is a neighbour, and her husband the landlord of the house. She said she would take care of it, and soon afterwards Mr Rothwell was informed where the dress was. Next morning she [Elizabeth] went to Mrs Greenhalgh for the dress, but to her astonishment, she denied all knowledge of it. On the afternoon of the same day, the dress was found in the cellar-hole, with three breadths of silk taken out of it. Several witnesses were found to prove the delivery of the dress to Mrs Greenhalgh. She was summoned before the magistrates who ordered

her to pay 15 shilling, the amount of the damage, and 14 shilling expenses. The circumstances which adds materially to the disgraceful character of the case, is that Rothwell, from a conscious feeling that the landlord ought not to suffer from an accident caused by his child, is actually rebuilding the cottage at his own expense from savings of several years, and what he can raise from his friends. It is a rare instance of sterling integrity, and ought to have met a better reward from whose property he is restoring from the fruits of his industry.

1886   The *Illustrated Police News* reported on a murder at Southport on 12 November. Sixteen-year-old Albert Smith had been a tram driver but was dismissed. He found accommodation at the house where 19-year-old Maud Hamilton lived with her wealthy mother. However, difficulties arose and the lad left the house. Soon afterwards the girl left home too – but she later returned, bringing Smith with her. On 12 November, Smith asked the girl to accompany him to the skating rink; she refused, locked herself in a cupboard, and refused to come out. In retaliation, Smith locked himself in his bedroom. The girl pleaded with him to let her in, and eventually the door was opened. Soon afterwards a shot was heard, and the servants found the girl lying on the floor, shot in the side. She was critically injured, but did say 'it was an accident and I love him' before she died. Smith was later found guilty of manslaughter and sentenced to six months' imprisonment.

27 NOVEMBER

A love affair ended in death at Southport in 1886.

1834   Times were tough for the handloom weavers; the burden of getting the cloth they wove back to the masters who brought them their 'pieces' often meant that the whole family became involved with the process. There were also penalties to be paid should he and his family not meet the targets. One Kirkham weaver named Thomas Nixon was committed to the house of correction for one month by Messrs Thomas Pate & Co. for 'returning work entrusted to him in an unfinished state'.

28 NOVEMBER

29 NOVEMBER **1874** An inquest was held at the White Lion Hotel at Clitheroe on the death of Susannah Ushers, a 49-year-old widow who was found dead in a field near Clitheroe Station. Thomas Cowporthwaite was charged with having caused her death. He and Thomas Scott were returning from Blackburn, where they had been to see the footraces, and Ushers (who was under the influence of alcohol) was in the same carriage. She became very familiar with Cowporthwaite and, on reaching Clitheroe, the two of them went down a country lane and entered a field, where they remained for some time. Cowporthwaite then came out of the field on his own. The day after, Ushers was found dead in the field, and her bonnet and veil were found 100 yards away. The jury returned a verdict to the effect that there was insufficient evidence to show how the deceased had met her death, even though Dr Musson attributed death to exposure to the cold. The deputy coroner, Mr Deane, denounced the way Cowporthwaite had acted, and the latter was then discharged.

The White Lion Hotel, where the inquest was held on the body of Susannah Ushers.

30 NOVEMBER **1835** Word soon spread to gamekeeper Joseph Wilson, employed by John Taylor of Moreton Hall and Mr Lomax of Clayton Hall, that some poachers were planning to take some prized game belonging to his masters; he was determined to put at stop to it. Wilson organised some assistance and, at about two o'clock on the moonlit morning, he set out to ambush the intruders. They crossed over Cock Bridge near Great

Harwood and entered the plantation there. Keeping a low profile, they soon came across four poachers armed with guns, near a place called The Holme, and confronted them. During the confusion that followed, shots were fired and Robert Howson – one of the gamekeeper's assistants – fell down dead, having been shot through the head by one of the poachers. In the midst of more disorder, the poachers made their escape. However, the evidence was already against them; they had been seen in a local beer shop at Great Harwood on the night in question, discussing their nocturnal gaming crimes. The local constables were quick to act, and arrested four men: Rowland Heald, Evan Brindle, Thomas Rushton and West Kenyon. The inquest into the death of Robert Howson was held at the Cock Inn, now the Game Cock Inn, at Great Harwood on 9 December 1835, where a verdict of 'wilful murder' was returned against the four poachers. Later, West Kenyon was prudent enough to turn 'King's Evidence'. The trial of the other three poachers took place on 29 March 1836, at Lancaster Assizes, before Judge Denman. It was a lengthy trial; the many witnesses, and the evidence of Kenyon, was more than enough to find Heald, Brindle and Rushton guilty. The jury was only out for half an hour before returning with the verdict of 'guilty' against all the prisoners, with a recommendation for mercy. No mercy was forthcoming from Lord Denman, however, who passed the death sentence upon all three accused and ordered for them to be executed the following day, and have their bodies buried in the confines of Lancaster Prison. However, before the judge left Lancaster Castle a few days later, he changed the sentence to transportation for life.

The aptly-named Cock Inn, now the Game Cock Inn, where the inquest was held on Robert Howson.

DECEMBER

FEARFUL MURDER NEAR WIGAN

The brutal attack on Catherine Houghton, and the murder of Annie Houghton. (*See* 17 December.)

1 DECEMBER   1871   There were reports that a boggart had been seen by the local residents at Kirkham and district. The ghostly being was said to have travelled around Kirkham, Westby, Wrea Green, Clifton and Newton. It was described as being tall in stature, and dressed sometimes as a man and sometimes as a woman. It became known as 'the man in women's clothing' and they gave it the name Margaret Henry. There were many accounts of strange knockings on doors and windows at night and early mornings. The farmers of the area were gratified to learn that many of their servants took to their beds early rather than roaming the streets – at least as long as the boggart was about.

2 DECEMBER   1851   A labourer named Joseph Hargreaves met his death when he was assisting an old man in removing some ashes in a hand cart from Poke Street (in Burnley) down to the river Brun. They were passing down Rodney Street, at a considerable incline, when the cart overpowered the old man; the shaft ran against Hargreaves' breast and jammed him against the wall. He was so seriously injured that he died almost immediately. An inquest held on the body later returned a verdict of 'accidental death'.

3 DECEMBER   1852   At 10.20 a.m., an explosion took place at the bleach-works of John Smith Junior & Co., when the boiler burst. The bleach-works was situated about 2 miles from Bolton and gave employment to around 180 hands. The boiler room stood in the centre of the works; to the left of this was the mangling house and on the right was an open yard. In front of the boiler house, 8-10 yards away, stood the wheelwright's shop; to the rear was the engine house with a condensing engine of 20hp. The report of the explosion was terrific, and was heard throughout the neighbourhood. The boiler (thought to weigh over 20 tons) was lifted from its bed and rolled into the yard – the engine house was blown down and the mangling house was completely destroyed. When the explosion occurred there were eighteen people in the mangling house, who were all covered with debris and scalded by the heated steam. Every assistance was rendered in the quickest possible time, but two men and a woman were brought out dead, and nine were seriously injured – one whose back was broken. Among the dead was William Lever, aged 57, who

The terrible boiler explosion at Bolton in 1852.

was married with five children – he was crossing the yard when he was struck; the upper part of his head was blown off. Michael Grant, aged 40, left a wife and family. He died soon after being removed from the rubble. The woman was named as being Jane Watson, aged 34; she was in the mangle house and was crushed and scalded to death. The injured included Joseph Greenhalgh, James Ashton, Isaac Entwistle, 17-year-old Mary Bent, John Daker – who was severely scalded, Harriet Aspinall, Mary Wood, John Lawton, John Crompton and Samuel Taylor.

1865 Stephen McEvoy, aged 60, lived at Park Street in Salford, next door to Jane Headon and her husband. Mrs Headon had a cat, which in the previous few days had gone missing; she was convinced that McEvoy had something to do with it. On 4 December 1865, she sent her husband round to McEvoy's house to question him about the cat, and, following a heated debate, McEvoy hit the husband on the head with a poker. Mrs Headon arrived to take her injured husband home but, as they were leaving, McEvoy aimed another blow at the injured man. He missed his target and instead struck Mrs Headon on the head with the poker. Mrs Headon was taken to the Infirmary where she had her wounds dressed. She seemed unaffected until Christmas Eve, when complications set in, and she died on 28 December. The defence questioned Mrs Headon's injuries and medical experts stated that the damage might have been caused by her banging her head against McEvoy's door. The jury found McEvoy guilty of manslaughter but recommended mercy on account of the provocation. The judge stated that he had no doubt that McEvoy was exasperated by Headon's conduct. He also said that he would take into account the jury's recommendation, but that it must be remembered that McEvoy had come to the door with a dangerous weapon in his hand. People had to be taught that when they used such weapons they were responsible for all of the consequences. Taking all the circumstances into consideration, the judge stated that he would only sentence McEvoy to six months' imprisonment.

1868 Forty-three-year-old Robert Caton, a plasterer of Garden Street, Preston, was out shopping with his daughter Ellen between seven and eight in the evening. Whilst they were in Mrs Gabbatt's shop in North Road, Mrs Caton came in; she was drunk and immediately started abusing her husband, both verbally and physically. The husband kept pushing her away, and eventually hit her and threw her out of the shop. Robert and Ellen then returned home, and a little while later the wife came in and started shouting and swearing at her husband again. Eventually, Robert went into the cellar and returned with a piece of wood about 2ft long, and struck his wife across her temple. His daughter Ellen tried to stop him, but she was pushed to one side and ran outside in fear. She returned a few minutes later and saw her father strike her mother three or four times; blood poured from her wounds. Robert then went to the Iron Duke public house on North Street and ordered several pints of ale. Mrs Caton's son (by a former husband) went into the house and found his mother dead on the sofa. Ellen was told to fetch her father at the Iron Duke and tell him that his wife was dead. When charged with the murder, he replied, 'I've done it – I've done it.' Caton was later brought before the magistrates and remanded on the charge of murder.

6 DECEMBER **1880** *Blackburn Times*, 6 December 1880:

The Swan & Royal, where the skeletal remains of an infant were found hidden in a wall in 1880.

A presumed murder, which no doubt will be shrouded in mystery until earthly judgement ceases has been brought to light in an extraordinary manner. Whilst a number of workmen were engaged in alterations at the Swan & Royal Hotel (Clitheroe) kept by Mr George Lofthouse, on Thursday, the contractor for the work Mr Joseph John Wilson, of York Terrace took down a partition in the front bedroom and discovered a cavity which contained in a bundle the remains of a human body. The skeleton was that of a very young, possibly a new born child, and the body, of which the bones were the only tangible

remains, had probably been hidden beneath the ceiling of the front bedroom and the floor of the upper storey. There was a vestige of matter left, which once might have been flesh, but all the bad smells which accompany decomposition had passed away. There was nothing beyond a checked handkerchief in which the bones were tied up to lead to identification. The tight manner in which the remains were tied up has given rise to the conjecture that the child was smothered, but it is quite possible that the crime may have been nothing more than concealment of birth. It is about forty years since any alterations were made in that part of the building where the skeleton was discovered and the general belief of those who are acquainted [with] the place is that the crime was committed so far back. It is certain that the body had completely decomposed and the bones dried and withered. Three years ago a workman who was putting gas fittings underneath the floor observed what he thought was a dirty rag and laid a pipe over it, never for a moment thinking that the rag contained a human skeleton. Dr Smithies who was called in to see the remains could not tell how long ago the crime was committed. It has been decided that it would be quite unnecessary to hold an inquest and the police have been given a warrant for the funeral.

1834 Eighteen-year-old Daniel Leech, along with several others, was 7 DECEMBER drinking at the Highland Lassie, a beer shop in Rochdale, when James Lord became abusive, and called Leech's sister some inappropriate names. Daniel Leech asked him to stop, but Lord took off his coat and threw a punch in Leech's direction – he missed his target. Leech jumped on to a nearby bench and, while Lord was still attacking, kicked him violently in the stomach. The kick was hard enough to rupture the intestines and Lord died the following day. At Lancaster Assizes in March 1835, Leech was found guilty of manslaughter under circumstances of great provocation.

1835 'Up and Down Fighting' was once common in Lancashire, 8 DECEMBER especially among the colliers in the mining districts; there were no rules, and the death of one of the opponents was more often the norm than the rarity. The *Preston Chronicle* reported this fight at Bolton in December 1835:

On Sunday morning week a young man aged 29, John Brigs was killed by fighting in a field near Bolton. An inquest was held on the body, when it appeared that the deceased was killed by a man named William Monks in a worrying match, or up and down fighting. The jury returned a verdict of 'Manslaughter' against Monks who was committed for trial at the next Liverpool Assizes.

9 DECEMBER 1886 *Mexico*, a German cargo ship, ran aground off the Lancashire coast in a storm; the lifeboats at Lytham, St Anne's and Southport scrambled to the scene. Spectators feared the worst when lights from the lifeboats stopped showing at sea – these fears were confirmed when bodies from the crew of the Southport lifeboats started to be washed ashore. At first light the Southport lifeboat *Eliza Fernley* was spotted keeled over on a sandbank. Next the St Anne's lifeboat *Laura Janet* was spotted overturned. Twelve members of the *Mexico* were eventually rescued by the Lytham lifeboat – but at great cost. Twenty-seven of the forty-four lifeboat men who set off that night had perished in the raging seas off the Lancashire coats – they left behind sixteen widows and fifty orphans. A wave of national sympathy followed and a relief fund was quickly organised. To mark the most tragic day in British lifeboat history, a number of monuments were set up to the disaster. On St Anne's promenade, the stone figure of a lifeboat man – dressed as he

The memorial on St Anne's promenade to the lifeboat disaster of 1886.

would have been at the time of the tragedy – stares out to the open sea where his comrades perished. The names of all who died are listed below it. Other monuments to the disaster are at St Anne's Church and Lytham Church, and at Duke Street Cemetery a communal grave for six members of the Southport crew is topped by a broken mast.

10 DECEMBER 1872 The first newspaper reports were coming in about a terrible accident which occurred the previous day at the new pit being sunk on the Gawthorpe estate at Habergham Eaves, near Burnley. The shaft had been sunk 240 yards, and on the day of the accident five men were

This memorial at the public cemetery on St Johns Road, Padiham, recalls the Habergham Colliery tragedy. The inscription reads: 'Richard Starkie of Sweet Home, who was killed at Habergham Colliery, Dec. 9th 872, aged 39 years.'

at the bottom of the pit walling up the shaft with bricks. A man at the top, George Cronshaw, was filling a wagon with bricks to send down to the men below; he pushed the wagon forward to the lip of the shaft – where there should have been a slide covering the shaft to prevent anything falling down. Unfortunately, the slide was not in place and he and the wagon went over the edge and plunged over 700ft into the darkness. There was nowhere to hide for those working below, and two of them were killed instantly by the falling wagon and the bricks; the other three were all hurt to some extent, one dying of his injuries later. Those who were killed were 50-year-old George Cronshaw, who left a wife and eight children, 30-year-old John Salkeld, who left a widow and two children, and 39-year-old Richard Starkie, who left a wife and five children.

11 DECEMBER   **1885**   As Mrs Bradley of Old Hall Street, Bolton, entered her chambers at about midnight, a man sprang at her from the darkness and began slashing at her throat with a razor. Hearing her screams, the servant girl rushed in – the attacker then turned his attention on her. Fortunately she was wearing a scarf, which saved her from any serious injuries. The commotion roused the next-door neighbours, but the stranger made his escape through a bedroom window and lowered himself to the floor by means of an outside projection. Mrs Bradley was seriously injured, but as the main artery was not severed she was expected to survive.

The servant girl probably saved the life of Mrs Bradley – but she too was attacked by the burglar at Old Hall Street, Bolton.

DESPERATE ATTEMPT AT DOUBLE MURDER – BOLTON

12 DECEMBER   **1857**   The *Preston Guardian* reported on the horrible child murder that took place at Poulton-le-Fylde on 6 December. Mrs Thompson and her servant girl Ellen Ingram came from Everton to Poulton on 24 November. The girl became ill and Mrs Thompson went to find a charwoman to do the housework. While she was away, Ellen gave birth to a child. On her return, Mrs Thompson called in the surgeon, Mr Bowness, who examined Ellen and accused her of just having given birth. At first the girl denied this, but eventually she admitted that she had had the child, wrapped it up in a blanket, and thrown it into the pit on the outskirts of town. The police dragged the pit for a number of hours, but to no avail. The same evening, the nurse Elizabeth Redshaw discovered the body of a female child at the foot of Ellen's bed – its throat had been cut from ear to ear. At the inquest, Ellen Ingram said, 'I have done a weary job. I cut its throat, it never screamed, but it stirred one hand. I was mad, or I would not have done it. I did it with a knife that Mrs Thompson bought.' She was then committed to the next Lancaster Assizes.

1860 Isabella Beck pleaded guilty at the Lancaster Assizes of child **13 DECEMBER** stealing at Bolton-le-Moors on 6 October. She was sentenced to fourteen days' imprisonment. On 9 October, a local joiner and auctioneer were returning from Highfield when they found the child lying beside the road on the moor. On taking it to the police, they found it to be the child of Mr Thomas, a moulder of 45 Bullock Street, Bolton-le-Moors. Mr Thomas, accompanied by a police officer, had just arrived in search of the child. Beck was captured the same evening by the police; she was about 20 years old and was said to have been a native of Lancaster.

1840 The *Preston Guardian* reported: **14 DECEMBER**

At the conclusion of a burial service in the churchyard at Burnley, an alarming accident occurred. Immediately contiguous to a grave in which a body this afternoon was deposited, there was a subterranean bone house, the arch of which rest upon a wall 18ft high, which descended from the north-east extremity of the churchyard to the bend of the river. The wall had been rendered insecure by the action of the water upon its foundations, and the consequence was that it gave way, and fell with a tremendous crash into the watercourse. The arch of the vault, upon which the mourners and others were standing, falling with it. There was a great scene of terror as living men and women found themselves mixed up with the remains of their ancestors – but fortunately nobody was hurt.

1832 A number of lads were playing football in a field at Gorton, **15 DECEMBER** Manchester, and – as is not uncommon – a dispute arose between two of the boys. William Horsfall and John Hibbert went beyond the verbal and commenced to fight. This went on for a few minutes until Hibbert got hold of his opponent, threw him down, and grasped him by the throat for about sixty seconds. Horsfall then put his hands up to signify that he had had enough, and then attempted to get up from the ground. Hibbert gave Horsfall a violent kick in the side of the body – with such force that it ruptured the boy's intestines. Help was soon at hand, but the poor lad expired the following day. An inquest was held on the body, and a verdict of 'manslaughter' was returned against Hibbert. Four other lads taken into custody at the same time were later released.

16 DECEMBER   1863   The *Preston Guardian* reported:

> One of the most melancholy occurrences we have had for some time to record took place at Warton, near Lytham, last evening, by which seven persons were drowned. For three weeks past there have been staying at Lytham, Mr Sagars, a merchant, of Manchester, together with his wife, two sons and three daughters. The sons, Henry and Thomas, were aged respectably 21 and 16 years – and the daughters, Jessie, Laura, and Mary were aged 21, 15, and 10 years old. During their visit at Lytham, Miss Eliza Wilson, a young lady of about 20 years, had been staying with them, and on Tuesday week the party were joined by Mr Walter Wilson, brother to Miss Wilson, aged 23, who, it is believed is betrothed to the eldest of the Misses Sagars. About seven o'clock on Tuesday morning all the party, with the exception of Mr and Mrs Sagars proceeded to the river for the purpose of hiring a boat, and shooting birds. None of the youths, it is believed, were accustomed to rowing, but as there was little wind blowing, although the tide was beginning to flow, no danger was apprehended. They stated to the owner of the boat, a man named Parkinson, that they intended pulling as far as the docks, and left with one pair of oars.
>
> Soon afterwards, two of the youths were seen on one of the sandbanks with their guns, but nothing more was heard of them until a telegram was received by Mr Sagars, stating that they had gone on to Preston with the tide, and would return to Lytham in time for dinner at six o'clock. As they did not arrive home at that hour, Mr and Mrs Sagars became very anxious, and a boat crew was despatched up the river in search of the party. But after proceeding as far as Naze Point, they had to return without any tidings of them, beyond what they had learned from the men on the dredger, who saw them passing homeward about half past five. At daybreak the following day, the search was renewed when the boat in which the missing party had left Lytham was discovered opposite Warton, and soon after the body of Miss Laura Sagars was found on the sands. All further search, on both the Lytham and Heasketh [*sic*] side of the estuary has so far proved fruitless. Of course nothing is known, and never can be known with certainty of the cause of the fearful casualty, but it is supposed that the boat's keel must have caught up in one of the net's stakes below Warton. If such were the case, as the tide was receding with great rapidity, the boat would have probably been instantaneously upset, and the whole engulfed without the least warning or hope of rescue.

17 DECEMBER   1868   Reports were made regarding a brutal murder which was committed on 15 December on a farmstead occupied by Joseph Roper at Ackton Hall, about 3 miles from Wigan. Roughly 200 yards away from the hall was a barn, converted for use by the farm bailiff William Houghton. At about 6.30 a.m. on 15 December, Houghton left his house and proceeded to Gathurst Station to meet Mr Roper. During this time, the barn dwelling was left in the charge of his eldest daughter, 12-year-old Annie. After an absence of about an hour and a half, Houghton and Roper returned along with a man named Parkinson, an underlooker at one of Mr Roper's pits. When they reached the pit, which stood a few yards from the door, Mrs Houghton saw something lying on the grass which, at that distance, looked like a few geese or ducks. On closer inspection, she found that it was the dead body of her poor girl Annie. The others rushed about looking for the other daughter, 9-year-old Catherine. Thankfully she was found, and soon in the arms of her parents. Catherine was able to give the following horrible account of what had happened. Soon after her father had left, a collier had appeared at the doorway and asked if William Houghton lived there. Annie had said that he did, but he was down at the hall; no sooner had she said this than the man raised a hammer and struck the girl on the forehead. Annie tried to run away, but the man kept beating her with the hammer, and, by the time the child reached the pit, he struck her once more with fatal consequences. The man returned to the house to seek out the other child, who he beat several times with the hammer, then took by the throat before throwing her over a hedge. There she remained, shivering with fright until her parents found her. The attacker then ransacked the house looking for something to steal, but only found a silver watch. Two younger children lay in bed upstairs, happily ignorant of what was happening below. An infant in a cradle in the kitchen was also left unharmed. A reward was offered for the capture of the murderer, and a man named Thomas Jones was later arrested in Yorkshire for the offence – but he was later discharged. As far as I am aware, no one was ever brought to justice for this horrible affair.

1834 An inquest was held at the Swan Inn in Colne on the death of 8-year-old Margaret Robinson, who was accidentally burnt at the house of her parents. Margaret was attended to by a man named William Lambert, who pretended to cure burns. She was considered to be doing very well until about a week previous, when Lambert applied something from a bottle on to the child's back. She immediately became distracted with pain, fell into a strong convulsive fit, and expired about two hours later. A verdict of 'manslaughter' was returned and Lambert was committed to the Lancaster Assizes.

18 DECEMBER

19 DECEMBER   **1850**   Reports were made of an old man who froze to death two weeks previous in a hedge near the Tandle Hills at Rochdale. The body was removed to the George & Dragon pub at Trub Smithy and was recognised as 71-year-old James Kershaw of Lower Place, Rochdale. The deceased had been missing since Thursday week, when he was last seen alive getting sticks near the place where his body was found.

20 DECEMBER   **1864**   Reports were made of a little girl named Eva Bowker, the daughter of 24-year-old Henry Bowker of Friday Street in Blackburn, who was burnt to death. The previous Wednesday at about eleven o'clock, the girl was seen running from her grandfather's house in Cook Folly with her clothes on fire and screaming in agony. Spectators ran to her aid and extinguished the flames, but not before the poor child was burnt all over her body. The infant stated that she had been sitting in front of the kitchen fire when her grandfather, without saying anything, had pushed her against the flames. He was an old imbecile named Benjamin Smith and the local children had been in the habit of tormenting him; it was thought that the injured child might have had something to do with the torment. Smith denied pushing her. The child lingered in great pain until the following Friday, when she died at noon.

21 DECEMBER   **1910**   The worst underground explosion in English coal mining history, in terms of lives lost, took place at Hulton Colliery, No. 3 Bank Pit, known locally as the 'Pretoria Pit', on the Atherton/Westhoughton border. Three hundred and forty-four men and boys perished instantly in the blast. Little wonder, then, that there were no carols that Christmas in Westhoughton and Atherton. Hardly a street in either village was unaffected by the disaster. One woman lost her husband and four sons; a retired collier lost five sons, a nephew and his brother. There were so many funerals over the next few weeks that churches and little chapels were packed to full capacity – and because of this, one young bride had to be married at five o'clock in the morning in order to be fitted in. In January, the rector at Sacred Heart's Church summed up the feelings of the villagers when he said:

> The hearses, the mourning coaches, the long funeral processions, and then throngs of bereaved widows and orphans, relatives and friends, the hundreds of visitors, all of them making their way to the last resting places. To see people in tears, to hear the sobbing and singing of the wives and children, brothers and sisters was something beyond human endurance.

This memorial to those who perished in the 'Pretoria Pit' explosion can be seen in Westhoughton Cemetery. (Jack Nadin)

He added at the end, 'No one will ever forget these sights.' Happily, no one has forgotten that dreadful day in December 1910, and each year a crowded memorial service takes place at Westhoughton. The year 2010 marks the 100th anniversary of the disaster; no doubt a special service will take place to honour the occasion.

1845 Newspaper agent Joseph Fielding was returning from the Middleton railway station at around 10.30 p.m. when, near the bottom of Tonge Springs, about 30 yards from the church, he was set upon by

22 DECEMBER

three men and knocked to the ground. The men kicked him severely and attempted to throw him into a river. The attackers took all of his money as well as two memorandum books. Fielding later said that the men were a 'rough-looking lot, and appeared like railway labourers', and one of them was wearing a light-coloured jacket.

23 DECEMBER 1894 A 25-year-old collier, James Waggstaff of Tyldesley, was not on the best of terms with his 11-year-old stepson William Henry Holmes, and he often ill-treated him. One day he saw the lad playing, and Waggstaff 'cuffed' him and led him away, saying that he was going to take the lad to his aunt's house. Two days later, Waggstaff reported the boy as missing. In the neighbourhood of Tyldesley were several disused coal shafts and a search was made of these. Waggstaff and a companion found the boy's body in an old shaft at the Peel Wood Pit. It later emerged that screams were heard coming from the old pit on the day that the lad was supposed to have disappeared. Waggstaff was later charged with murdering him, but at the hearing in March 1895 he was discharged, and a verdict of 'wilful murder against some person unknown' was returned.

24 DECEMBER 1845 It was around 7.45 p.m. on Christmas Eve 1845 as Thomas Sweeting, a waggoner employed by Mary Broadbent & Son, manufacturers of Hopwood Mill in Oldham, was returning home from Manchester. His wagon was heavily laden and he was gleefully looking forward to the forthcoming merriments of Christmas. As he approached the junction of the Lees and Greenacres Moor Road, he slipped whilst going into the main road; before he could recover himself, the wheel of the wagon went over his head. He was so severely injured that he died within a few minutes of being taken into the surgery of Mr Earnshaw. The deceased had not been long employed as a driver, and was around 71 years of age. He left a grown-up family to mourn his loss.

25 DECEMBER 1834 A barbarous murder was committed in Atherton Street, Liverpool by a man named Peter Taylor, who had recently been appointed cook on the ship *Barnster*. Having gone to a house of ill repute in Atherton Street – a part of town infested with brothels – the man met a 25-year-old woman named Mary Anne Benson, one of the wretched creatures who lived in the house. After having a small altercation with the girl, he suddenly pulled out a clasp knife and plunged it into the girl's breast; she immediately expired. The murderer then tried to make his escape and hurried towards the dock to board his ship, which was due to sail the very next day. However, the alarm was given and the watch was sent in pursuit; Taylor was captured before he boarded the ship, and duly charged with the murder.

1876 An inquest was held at the Rostron Arms in Edenfield, near Rawtenstall, touching the death of a young man named Richard Thornley, who was run over by the fire engine. A verdict of 'accidental death' was recorded.

The Rostron Arms, where the inquest was held on Boxing Day in 1876 on the body of Richard Thornley.

1892 There was a skating disaster in Rochdale. Around 200 people were enjoying skating on the ice of the frozen lodge at Marlands Dyeworks; among them were Nelly Holt and Ernest Wild. The pair were about 12 yards from the edge of the lodge when the ice broke and they were plunged into the icy waters. Nelly was an expert swimmer and managed to grab hold of the ice, but it kept breaking. Her cousin Charles Coates, seeing her struggle, skated over and then crawled on his hands and knees towards her. He threw the end of his overcoat to her, but at this point the ice broke beneath him and both cousins disappeared underwater. They were not seen again until their bodies were recovered some three hours later. It was only by sheer good luck that others did not lose their lives. Lucy Holt, seeing her sister Nelly in the water, tried to save her – but she too fell in. At one point almost a dozen rescuers were in the water. Some men on the banks tore down fencing from the hedges and threw them into the water, and by this means some were saved. With ropes, boats and quickly-made rafts, others were also saved. However, four died. They were Edwin Blackburn, Ernest Wild, Charles Coates and Nelly Holt.

1875 There was a fatal boiler explosion at the workhouse in Fulwood, Preston, which resulted in the death of 7-year-old John Longley. It was

John's job to light the boilers, which were there to heat the pipes of the classrooms; he did this every morning at eight o'clock. The boiler exploded just before ten o'clock. Little John was still down in the boiler house when this happened, and when found he was under a mass of steel, stones and brick, and was horribly mutilated. The rest of the children, who had just begun to move into the classrooms, escaped. Two little boys were scalded by the hot steam, but they were expected to recover. There was severe condemnation at the inquest that the important task of lighting boilers should be assigned to one so young.

29 DECEMBER   **1895**   Joseph Ellis Jones, a labourer, was tried at the Manchester Assizes for the murder of Michael M'Donough at Standish, near Wigan. He was found guilty of manslaughter at the trial in March 1896. M'Donough lodged with Jones and, on 29 December 1895, both returned home in a drunken state. Jones would not let M'Donough into the house, but the latter broke in and attacked him. During the struggle, Jones grabbed M'Donough by the scarf he was wearing and drew it so tight that it throttled the man to death. In his defence, Jones stated that he was only doing what was required to protect himself. After finding him guilty of manslaughter, the jury added a rider that the crime was committed under great provocation and the sentence was deferred.

30 DECEMBER   **1831**   An inquest was held at Kirkby, Lonsdale, upon the body of John Baines of Barbon, a shoemaker who had dropped down in the street on the previous Sunday night. The unhappy man had apparently been drinking to excess during the evening, and a verdict to the effect that he died from intoxication was returned.

31 DECEMBER   **1858**   A number of men of the 100th Dublin Militia, stationed at Burnley Barracks, went on a drunken riot in the town centre. Being pay day, the soldiers had spent a great deal of time in the local inns. The windows of the Thorn Hotel were broken, as well as several panes of the smoking room windows at the Bull Inn. One gentleman sitting there narrowly missed injury – or even death – as a bayonet was thrust through the window. A young man, Nick Barrett, was stabbed in the shoulder while walking along Yorkshire Street and a collier walking close by was cut around the head, thigh, and body. At John Berry's butchers shop on Yorkshire Street, all the windows were smashed. One of the inhabitants there was forced to take refuge upstairs but was followed by the militia, who thrust bayonets into the door. Another man was stabbed on New Market Street and was left in a pool of blood. The conduct of the militia was described as being 'perfectly wild'; they howled like animals and stuck their bayonets into anything that happened to be in range. One even sharpened his bayonet on a doorstep and called for others to do the same, shouting, 'Let's give it to the English B******s.' Other soldiers of a different regiment were dispatched from the barracks – and finally all of the rioters were rounded up. However, after the disgraceful conduct, 200 residents of the town marched up Westgate towards the barracks armed with bludgeons, axes and other weapons, intent on revenge. The local magistrates, Mr Handsfield and Mr Carrswell, were soon on the scene and were able to dissuade the residents from going further. The soldiers were confined to barracks for days afterwards, and many suffered disciplinary action, but it was several days before the residents of Burnley finally calmed down.

BIBLIOGRAPHY

Baggoley, Martin, *Foul Deeds and Suspicious Deaths in Manchester*, Wharncliffe Books, 2004

Brabin, Angela, *The Black Widows of Liverpool: A Chilling Account of Cold-Blooded Murder in Victorian Liverpool*, Palatine Books, 2003

Cole, John, *Foul Deeds and Suspicious Deaths in and around Rochdale*, Wharncliffe Books, 2007

Dixon, G.M., *Folk Tales and Legends of Old Lancashire*, Minimax Books Ltd, 1991

Evans, Graham, *The Fylde: Places, Legends and Tales*, Creek Publishers, 1989

Eyre, Kathleen, *Lancashire Legends*, Dalesman Books, 1972

Fairhurst, James, *Wigan's Worst Victorian Murders*, 2001

Fielding, Steve, *Hanged at Manchester*, The History Press, 2008

Fletcher, Mike, *Foul Deeds and Suspicious Deaths in Wigan*, Wharncliffe Books, 2007

Greenhalgh, Steve, *Foul Deeds and Suspicious Deaths in Blackburn and Hyndburn*, Wharncliffe Books, 2002

Harland, John, *Legends and Traditions of Lancashire*, 1873

Hassal, Keith and Firth, Mike, *Haunted Halls of Lancashire*, self-published, 1990

Holding, David, *Murder in the Heather: Being an Account of the Winter Hill Murder of 1838*, Friends of Smithills Hall, 1991

Hough, Peter, *Supernatural Lancashire*, Robert Hale Ltd, 2003

Howarth, Ken, *Ghosts, Traditions and Legends of Old Lancashire*, Sigma Leisure, 1993

Johnson, Keith, *Chilling True Tales of Old Preston*, Owl Books, 1990

McEwen, Alan, *Historic Steam Boiler Explosions*, Sledgehammer Engineering Press Ltd, 2009

Nadin, Jack, *Lancashire Mining Disasters 1835-1910*, Wharncliffe Books, 2006

Pearce, Joseph, *Lancashire Legends*, C. Wilson, 1947

Wright, Geoff, *Foul Deeds and Suspicious Deaths around Southport*, Wharncliffe Books, 2008